Seig ?

for

S & C

10593438

Book of Comfort

Alvin N. Rogness

AUGSBURG Publishing House • Minneapolis

BOOK OF COMFORT

Copyright © 1979 Augsburg Publishing House

Library of Congress Catalog Card No. 78-66943

International Standard Book No. 0-8066-1677-6

Scripture quotations unless otherwise noted are from the Revised Standard Version of the Bible, copyright 1946, 1952, and 1971 by the Division of Christian Education of the National Council of Churches.

Permission to quote from the following has been granted by the publishers: *Travels with Charlie* by John Steinbeck, by permission of Viking Penguin Inc. Will Durant article, copyright 1978 Saturday Review. All rights reserved.

Illustrations provided by Koechel Design
Artists: Chris Wold and Patsy Flaherty

MANUFACTURED IN THE UNITED STATES OF AMERICA

Contents

Preface

You and I are on a road of sharp turns and sudden dips. And there's fog, thick fog. Sometimes boulders block the way. We neglect the map and are lured into detours. Weary, we may want to give up. We cry for comfort.

There is comfort. Years ago God said,

> Comfort, comfort my people. . . .
> Speak tenderly to Jerusalem, and cry to her
> that her warfare is ended,
> that her iniquity is pardoned,
> that she has received from the Lord's hand
> double for all her sins.

God yearns to comfort us—but on his terms and in his way. If I call on God, I understand that he may have to stop me in my tracks and turn me around before he can be gentle. He may have to use the scalpel before he can heal my pain.

In these short chapters I've tried to describe stretches along the road. I've traveled many of them. I'm old enough to have learned a little about them. But I'm no heroic traveler. Many times I've rejected God's comfort and tried to go it alone. Often I've been puzzled about the kind of comfort he seemed to give.

I have the map, the Word of God, his wisdom and his promises. And I have a Friend who has walked the way before me and who walks with me now. His hand is on me to lead me and to hold me. There is no greater comfort than that.

When Memories Haunt You

My life is full of memories. The good ones make up a company of cherished people and events of the past that, added to the present, give my life fullness.

The bad ones add a touch of sadness and melancholy. But they don't haunt me or crush me. I have learned how to deal with them. I could never have done it without God.

There are three kinds of bad memories. First, memories of unpleasant or even tragic events over which I had no control. Second, memories of wrongs done to me by others. And third, memories of wrongs I have done to others, or of the good I have failed to do for them.

The first kind of memory is not destructive, because such memories carry no guilt. A tornado or a fire destroys your home. The fluctuation of the market wipes out your assets. Diabetes claims your leg. An accident kills your friend. These traumatic events leave you struggling to get your bearings, but they are simply part of the human situation. You did not cause them. You need feel no remorse.

Memories of wrongs done to you by others may be more troublesome. Someone you loved rejected you. Your partner in business maneuvered you out of your holdings. Someone you had trusted sued you unjustly. You may have trouble erasing the memory and ridding yourself of bitterness, but the wrong was someone else's, not yours.

The memories of your own wrongs are the destructive ones. Try as you will to marshal extenuating circumstances to excuse yourself, you won't succeed. Try to push the memories under the rug and forget them—they creep out to haunt you at the most unexpected moments. They demand that you deal with them.

If the people you have wronged are alive and within reach, you may make a direct approach. You may ask forgiveness and make what amends you can. If they are willing to accept your remorse and your efforts to mend the wrong, there will be healing. But often there's a roadblock. They cannot accept your pleas, or won't. The damage may be beyond repair. A man who has abandoned his family may never, try as he will, heal the wounds he has caused. A drunken driver cannot restore the life she crushed on the road. Every one of us has left a trail of wrongs, big and small, both by what we have done and by what we have failed to do. We will never be able to clear the road of all the debris. If we are sensitive at all, we carry a cargo of memories that threaten to crush us.

Unless—unless there is a place where we can dump the whole wretched load. And there is. That's where God comes in. Resting the load with him is not a "cop-out." It's rather as if a person has all sorts of bills hanging over him, and he goes to the bank and gets one loan and his new debtor (the bank) enables him to come to terms with all the others. This may be an inadequate parallel, but the Lord's sweeping forgiveness is just this kind of miracle.

There will be dangling ends, hurts that will never be healed until we die. But at the center of life, at the heart of the universe, in him who gave us life—the whole sorry stuff is removed as far as the east is from the west. We have the staggering assurance, "Your sins will I remember no more." And the memories we carry will have lost their power to destroy us. Moreover, we will have not only the right, but the duty, to forget them too!

In his *Macbeth,* Shakespeare has Lord and Lady Macbeth murder Duncan, the king. In the aftermath, Lady Macbeth's conscience drives her mad. Lord Macbeth comes to the doctor with the plea,

> Canst thou not minister to a mind diseased,
> Pluck from the memory a rooted sorrow,
> Raze out the written troubles of the brain,

And with some sweet oblivious antidote
Cleanse the stuffed bosom of that perilous stuff
That weighs upon the heart?

The doctor says, "More needs she the divine than the physician. God, God forgive us all!"

All the frantic distractions we contrive, all the skills of the psychologist, all the sedation of alcohol and drugs cannot remove the memories of our wrongs. There is no sweet oblivious antidote to cleanse the stuffed bosom of the perilous stuff of guilt—except the miracle of God's forgiveness in Christ and the cross.

The profound secret of this healing is the fact that all wrongs against other people are finally wrongs against the God who gave us life and who redeems us. King David committed adultery with Uriah's wife Bathsheba and engineered Uriah's death. When brought to repentance, David cried to God, "Against thee, thee only, have I sinned, and done that which is evil in thy sight." He could not bring Uriah back to life; he would make no amends by abandoning Bathsheba. There was but one place where he could find healing—in the mercy of God.

You don't play the coward and pass the buck when you bring your wretched memories and guilt to the foot of the cross. The Lord himself invites you to leave them there. You will still have scars, but the festering wounds will be gone. You stand before God as if you had never sinned. Finally, you are free to bask in all the good memories you have. And you have many!

When Suffering Seems Meaningless

Life is a jigsaw puzzle, a jumble of pieces that, try as we will, we'll never quite assemble into a clear picture. Most difficult to fit are the dark fragments of pain and evil and suffering. We wonder, Why are they needed at all? Has some impish elf smuggled them in to sabotage all attempts to make life meaningful?

We can understand suffering that comes directly from our wrongs or neglects. If I rob a bank and go to prison, if I betray a trust and lose my job, if I get drunk and drive off the road and languish in a hospital—these I can understand. But pain and tragedy sometimes have no clear connection with anything a person does or fails to do.

Why should my brother and his wife lose their Jimmy at 14 and their Dianne at 17 from brain tumors? Why should it have been our son who at 24 was struck down in a street accident? Why should my friend's lovely daughter become emotionally unbalanced and take her life just before her baby was to be born, and my cousin's brilliant son, in his first year at the university, lose his bearings and commit suicide? Why does a tornado destroy one farm and not another? Why should a hundred villages be devastated by a tidal wave?

Suffering strikes with reckless caprice. Many of the pieces simply do not fit. Job couldn't make them fit—remember? In what is perhaps the profoundest treatment of evil or suffering in all the world's literature, the Old Testament tells of this upright man who, in a swift succession of catastrophes, loses his property, his children, and his health. At first he's able to say "The Lord gave, and the Lord has taken away; blessed be the name of the Lord."

But as his pain continues, he begins to despair.

> Why was I not as a hidden untimely birth, as infants that never see the light? . . . I am alloted months of emptiness, and nights of misery are apportioned to me. . . . The night is long, and I am full of tossing till the dawn.

Then he begins to address God,

> Thy hands fashioned and made me; and now thou
> dost turn about and destroy me. . . . Why didst
> thou bring me forth from the womb? Would that
> I had died before any eye had seen me.

The amazing thing about Job is that, while challenging
God to give him some answer, he retains a rugged integrity.

> As long as my breath is in me . . . my lips will
> not speak falsehood, and my tongue will not utter
> deceit. . . . Till I die I will not put away my in-
> tegrity from me. I hold fast my righteousness, and
> will not let it go; my heart does not reproach me
> for any of my days.

This remarkable drama ends with Job still asking for
an answer, but with his trust in God unshaken.

One might try being indifferent to pain. Many schools
of thought—the Stoics of old, some Oriental cults, and
to a degree Christian Science—have advocated this path.
But if you deny pain in yourself, you must deny it in
others, and the springs of compassion dry up. Most of us
will not settle for that. We insist on trying to fit the pieces
somewhere, to find some meaning. Or, failing to fit them
anywhere, we will at least want to rescue some significance,
or if not significance, some value.

The Book of Job does give one very important clue.
God allows suffering, but he does not design it. He did
not arrange to have our son killed. He did allow it. Why
he allowed it, perhaps I will learn when I get to heaven,

but surely not before. But it helps me to know that he did not engineer the accident.

Since God keeps me in the dark about the riddle of evil and suffering, the best I can do is to struggle with what I might do about it. Do I shake my fists at God, do I throw up my hands, do I collapse in sheer weariness? Or do I dig around in the debris and try to find something that can be rescued?

I'd rather explore what can be salvaged. I can think of at least three ways to find meaning in suffering.

The first is the way my brother dealt with the death of his two children. He pointed to the obvious gain. God gave him and Ruth the joy of their children for a total of 31 years. Would they in their deepest grief ever wish that they had never had them, so they could be spared their present pain? No. Moreover, he asked, isn't death but an incident, a small punctuation mark, in the larger dimensions of a life that is eternal? Despite their great grief, they had been able to find a place for the dark pieces of the puzzle.

Second, suffering may have a good effect on the person who suffers. The Jewish people have known great suffering, and it is not uncommon for Jewish parents to acquaint their children early with the long history of the sufferings of their people—to prepare them for a similar fate, and, even more, to make them sensitive to the suffering of others. A tradition among the rabbinic schools of the Jewish people holds that only those who have known suffering themselves can understand and help those who suffer. We are not fully human until we have known suffering.

I am unable to tell whether the death of our Paul has made us more understanding of those who suffer. I think so. The bitterness I first felt I believe is gone, and I think we're better able "to weep with those who weep." If so, then the death of our son has had meaning.

The third way to make suffering meaningful is more mysterious. Pope John XXIII, when struck with cancer, offered his sufferings "for the peace of the world." He regarded his pain as a gift he had to give to all humanity. I am intrigued by this idea. Can those who suffer make of the very sufferings something good? If those who suffer do not protest and rebel, but accept pain as part of the human situation, can they give their gift to all people as an offering for the betterment of the world?

As members of the human family, we are not to be spared pain. We are not aristocrats, with an inalienable right to be happy. What the rest of the family suffers, you and I ought to suffer, to be part of them.

I am struck by these lines in Hebrews 12: "[Consider Jesus,] who for the joy that was set before him endured the cross, despising the shame, and is seated at the right hand of the throne of God. . . . You have not yet resisted [suffered] to the point of shedding your blood."

If you feel sorry for yourself, says this writer in Hebrews, take a look at Jesus. He deserved no suffering, yet he suffered. You're no better than he. Somehow his suffering has ennobled the whole world. You and I suffering with him, with his absence of bitterness, may in some way also help to ennoble the world. We cannot approach his matchless patience, but we are invited to try.

We in America have been spared the colossal sufferings of other nations in this volcanic century. None of our cities are in rubble, our borders have not been invaded, we are not homeless refugees. Why have we been spared? That too is a part of the puzzle. Certainly not because we are such virtuous, self-denying people. Who among us dares to claim special rights before God?

If our lives have fallen on pleasant times, and if we have been spared tragedies that have fallen on others, are we not the more under obligation to serve those who have dark pieces in their lives?

The puzzle is still here. Why suffering, why pain, why evil, why death? Instead of being paralyzed by the puzzle, instead of giving up and throwing the dark pieces away, we are invited to lift our eyes to God.

We will have to wait for the final answers, but meanwhile God will help us find some place for the pieces.

When Death Is at the Door

"I'll never be afraid of death again," he said, and then added, "but you'll never know how wonderful it is just to be alive." We hadn't seen each other since he had recovered from the heart attack that the doctors had predicted would be fatal. I saw in him new serenity and new joy.

He had always been a man of faith, but, like most of us, he had not yet called on his faith in the face of imminent

21

death. Now he knew what faith could do. He had passed the test, and his fear was gone.

I've been a bit puzzled, and not a little amused, at our recent preoccupation with "death and dying." Schools have courses of study on the subject, hospitals have workshops, congregations have series of talks. Usually a doctor, a lawyer, a funeral director, and a pastor are called in for their views—as if, once you have put it together from these several perspectives, you're ready to go.

I'm not cynical about these studies. The doctor can detail the scientific story of death, the lawyer can tell you how to put your financial house in order, the funeral director can prepare you for some practical chores that will face your family. All this may help get you ready for the exit, and even give you some degree of comfort.

But death is the one experience in life which is different from all others. There's no rehearsal before the play is on. And, no matter how well you put your house in order by arranging your finances and even being reconciled to those you've wronged, it's what lies after death that cries for an answer. As Shakespeare's Hamlet says:

> The undiscovered country, from whose bourn
> No traveler returns, puzzles the will,
> And makes us rather bear those ills we have
> Than fly to others that we know not of.

Of course there's much comfort in thinking that you have done everything to make it easier for your family when you're gone. I pay $50 a year for an insurance policy that will yield my family $150,000 if I die in an airplane accident, and I must admit that when the flight is rough, I sit back and am comforted, knowing that if I die my family will have more security than from my modest savings. And certainly, if you've been at odds with someone, there's comfort in becoming reconciled and having that dangling end tied up again.

But you expect to meet God on the other side. To come to terms with him is infinitely more important than to wrap up everything on this side.

A dying friend said, "Al, I'm not afraid to die, but I'm afraid to meet God, and you'll have to help me." He was a jurist, and it seemed absurd to him that God could forgive him and accept him in mercy. He said, "That's neither fair nor decent. We wouldn't handle wrongs in the lowest court of the land in such a shabby way." He felt that some sort of purgatory, either on this side or on the other side, would be necessary before God could accept him.

When at last the Lord overwhelmed him with the sheer mercy of grace in Christ Jesus, it was as a dawn of a new day for him. But his legal intuition was right. It isn't just, or even decent, for God to brush aside our wretched records and accept us in mercy. It is an act of pure love.

You'll never be able to gather up all the loose ends of your life and put them in order before you die. Get set as you will, something from the past will always haunt you. If there were no place to put the tangled snarls of your life, you'd be in trouble. But there is a place. God has provided it for you. It is at the foot of the cross, where Jesus Christ died for your sins, removing them "as far as the east is from the west."

Every one of us has a deep need for a place to rest, for someone to receive us "just as I am, without one plea, but that thy blood was shed for me, and that thou bidst me come to thee. . . ." The need is never greater than when we face the hour of death.

Instinctively we know that it will be absurd for us to stand before the high court of God and ask for justice: "Give me what I have coming, no more and no less." Before that bench each of us will have but one cry, "God be merciful to me, a sinner."

Most of you, from the time you were children, have heard the story of God's mercy in Christ. But you may never have really understood the radical character of the story. You have felt that somehow, some way, you will have to prove yourself with God before he'll take you in.

Now comes the hour of death. You know you haven't succeeded. There's too much unfinished business, too many dangling threads, too many neglects, too many hurts. Given a hundred years more, you still could not prove yourself before God.

You don't need to. God becomes not a judge, but a good and loving parent with a home waiting for you. All death can do is to open the door.

I like these lines from George Macdonald's *Diary of an Old Soul*.

Yestereve, Death came, and knocked at my thin door.
I from my window looked: the thing I saw,

The shape uncouth, I had not seen before.
I was disturbed—with fear, in sooth, not awe. . . .
I was like Peter when he began to sink.
To thee a new prayer therefore I have got—
That, when Death comes in earnest to my door,
Thou wouldst thyself go, when the latch doth click,
And lead him to my room, up to my cot;
Then hold thy child's hand, hold and leave him not,
Till Death has done with him for evermore.

When You Can't Forgive Yourself

N.B.

God can forgive you. Other people can forgive you. Do you ever have the right to forgive yourself?

If you mean to find excuses for yourself, no, you don't have that right. The shame is yours to bear. Try as you will, you can't erase something wretched in the past and pretend that it never happened. You are a responsible human being, and you can't pass the buck to God or to others.

That doesn't mean that you have to be weighed down

or crushed by the past. You place the past in God's hands, and God forgives. But neither God's forgiveness nor the forgiveness of others will alter the past. You'll have to live with its sadness. To pretend that it never happened is to escape into fantasy, and there's no healing in that.

Once forgiven by God (and by others, if possible), you have a duty to let the past be the past. You neither honor God nor help yourself by pulling the past into the present and rehearsing what can't be changed. God says, "Your sins will I remember no more." God forgets them, wipes them away as if they had never happened. What God can do, you cannot do. You cannot blot out your memories. They'll be like a cloud of hovering melancholy, but they need not be a load on your back. God tells you to "lay aside every weight . . . and run the race."

A pastor heard the anguished confession of a woman who had been unfaithful to her husband. He gave her the absolution, God's assurance of forgiveness in Christ. Upon leaving, she asked, "Shall I tell my husband?" He answered, "What is there to tell? It's all gone." He was saying that God had forgiven and forgotten, and the sin was obliterated. No need to tell. She too had a duty to forget. And you do too.

There is no way to be rid of the burden of remorse but to give it all to God. Even King David, who had committed adultery with Bathsheba and had murdered her husband Uriah, discovered that he couldn't brush it aside.

> When I declared not my sin, my body wasted away
> through my groaning all day long.

> For day and night thy hand was heavy upon me. . . .
> I acknowledged my sin to thee. . . .
> Then thou didst forgive the guilt of my sin.

The memory no doubt was with him until he died. But he went on, with God's forgiveness and blessing, to be Israel's greatest king.

If God couldn't use people with sad memories, or bless them, there'd be no one to use. Peter denied Christ, and other disciples abandoned him in the crisis. St. Augustine wasted years in debauched youth.

To remember the sins of the past, sad as they may be, is also to be on the alert to avoid them in the future. They act as radar, setting off the danger signal as new temptations loom.

We may try other ways than God's way, but they won't work. It won't do to say "everybody does it, so I'm no worse than others." You can't commit adultery and get any genuine comfort in knowing others who do. You can't cheat on a contract or on your income tax and find consolation in knowing others cheat too. Nor can you lose your temper and speak cruel words to someone you love and brush it aside with, "Well, that's the way I am." You have generated memories that will clamor for some place to rest. They will roam your soul like ghosts until you put them in the only place that can divest them of their power —before the cross of Christ.

Don't talk about forgiving yourself. Let God do the forgiving. Then go on to face the present and the future in the promises of God's comfort and blessing.

When You're Troubled about Miracles

Did Jesus actually walk on the Sea of Galilee? Did he change water into wine at Cana? Did he instantly heal the 10 lepers? Did he raise Lazarus from the dead?

These questions may trouble us in a scientific age. We've discovered the amazing orderliness of the universe, and it offends our reason to think that the God who gave us this gift of order would violate the gift. Some mischievous spirit perhaps, but God, oh no!

Most people who even bother to be troubled about miracles are willing to believe that God created the universe and that the man Jesus of Nazareth is God the Son come to earth. In a sense, they believe the two gigantic miracles (creation and incarnation) and are disturbed by the trivial ones.

How do we define a miracle? Something extraordinary for which there seems to be no scientific or rational explanation, like a person recovering from cancer when the doctors had given up? Or anything that baffles the imagination?

If my great-grandmother should return to earth for a week, her head would be swimming with the extraordinary —the miracles of the telephone, automobile, airplane, television, penicillin. These have become commonplace for us. If in wonder she should exclaim, "What has God done!" we might be startled out of our complacency to echo her question, "Yes, indeed, what amazing things hasn't God done with the knowledge he has given us?" After all, who put all these things in the universe, and who gave us probing minds to ferret them out? Are they any less miraculous or even mysterious because we find ways to explain them?

We are impoverished and dull if we fail to stand in wonder and awe at the staggering mystery of the ordinary. The daily conversation you have with a friend should send your little mind into orbit. Your brain sends impulses to the complicated machinery of your tongue and lips and diaphragm, and it produces sound waves. These waves strike your friend's eardrum and are translated into sound he hears, which in turn is transmitted to his brain as idea and meaning. If you're looking for something baffling, you need look no further.

Are biblical miracles so different? George Macdonald makes a delightful observation about Jesus changing water into wine at the wedding in Cana. He reminds us that every year God takes the seed of the grape and soil and sunshine and water (and a few weeks of time) and changes the water into wine—so why can't God compress the process into a moment of time? Why can't God have the ordinary become the extraordinary without annulling the orderliness of the universe and leaving us in chaos?

Even with the enormous explosion of knowledge in the last two centuries, the vast unknown (and perhaps unknowable) remains, giving us enough humility not to try to read the mind of God.

If you rest back in faith to believe that God created the universe (and you) and that Jesus of Nazareth is God come to earth to save us, then put the question of biblical miracles on the back shelf. Don't let these little, disturbing sideshows rob you of the big tent.

When You're Sick

I had usually thanked God for health and prayed that he might keep me from being ill. One evening in 1962, while speaking in a church, I suddenly collapsed. For two weeks I rested in a hospital waiting for my duodenal ulcer to stop bleeding.

I don't remember thinking that if I had stronger faith the bleeding would stop, or that someone with the gift of healing could lay hands on my head and make it stop. I relied on the skills that the Lord had given his servants, the doctors, and on the recuperative powers God had placed in my body. Of course I prayed for healing. Who doesn't when ill? You may have forgotten to pray for almost anything, but you do look to God when illness strikes. Even people who have trouble taking God's intervention seriously at all will pray in a crisis. From World War I came the refrain, "There are not atheists in foxholes." There is an old Russian proverb *Kak trevoga, tak do boga*—"In dire extremity man remembers his God."

I had no trouble thanking God for restoring my health, and I didn't bother my mind about whether it was through the science of medicine (which is God's) or through the healing powers of my body (which is God's), or whether God intervened in some special way.

Most of us will not exclude God's activity in medicine. It has always seemed to me that Jehovah's Witnesses and Christian Scientists limit God, denying part of the divine greatness and goodness.

God is on the side of life and health. If I understand Scripture right, God intended us for everlasting life, uninterrupted by death. God did not want us to be sick and die. Sin and sickness and death are intruders. I've never hesitated to urge the sick to pray for health. I think we're on God's side when we do everything possible to guard the gift of life and health.

God's plan is that sin and illness and death will at last be destroyed. Until that moment comes, God allows death to be the gateway through which we pass to inherit a life that is unending. We have no guarantee that we will outmaneuver death and live forever on this side, no matter how many healers we employ. Even Jesus, who brought back from the dead Lazarus, the widow's son at Nain, and Jairus' daughter, did not give them eternal tenure on this side. Eventually they did have to die.

Think of the comfort of healing God has given us in the last century through the spectacular advances in medical science. Many of the old killers—smallpox, diphtheria, peritonitis, pneumonia—are virtually gone.

Most doctors will say that they only remove or correct obstructions that keep the body from doing its own healing work. But often we don't cooperate with God in allowing the recuperative powers of our own bodies to take effect. We overeat. We drink damaging beverages. We fail to exercise.

In 1962 I took stock of my neglects. I had plunged ahead in my work, been neglectful of rest and sleep, and in other ways ignored the rights of my body. How could I expect God to keep me well if I defied his laws?

How about God's direct intervention through extraordinary means? Are there "divine healers"? The New Testament seems to indicate that God does give the gift of healing to certain people. And many people are sure that the Lord has, through these people, intervened in ways beyond the reach of science or the normal recuperative powers of the body.

When one of my friends was ill with a puzzling disease, people urged his wife to summon Oral Roberts or some person with a reputation for healing. She hesitated to summon anyone. Hundreds, even thousands of people were already pleading with God for his healing. She asked herself, What kind of a God would ignore the prayers of thousands and sit unmoved in his heavens, withholding healing till some "assigned" person came? She said, "I'd have to change my whole idea of a merciful God if I were to think that he would let my husband die unless a 'special' person prayed."

On the other hand, there is the testimony of many people who believe firmly that God has used some person (not the doctor) for special healing. Perhaps this is one of the mysteries we'll have to live with.

Much as we desire healing and life, we must try to keep illness in the right perspective. We know that life on this side is uncertain. We know too that the excellence of a life is not measured by its length, any more than the excellence of a painting depends on the size of the canvas. We live in the anticipation of life everlasting on the other side, which a gracious God in love and forgiveness has promised us in Christ Jesus.

To be sick puts you on trial. To be on your back in the hospital, in pain and perhaps with scant hope of recovery, is the hardest assignment life has given you. If you are able to exercise patience, love, cheerfulness, a sense of humor, and hope in such an hour, you may have given your family and friends the most treasured memories they'll ever have. If God can help you do that, your measure of comfort will be sublime.

When Prayers Go Unanswered

If you were headed in the wrong direction, on a road where a bridge had been washed out by a raging torrent, you wouldn't expect God to help you get there. You could rather count on God putting every possible roadblock in the way so that, discouraged, you'd turn around.

We often make the mistake of calling on God to comfort us in what we are doing, when above all else he wants to disturb us. He would be less than a loving God if he didn't.

God's stake with each of us is to shape us up into the kind of people we ought to be as his children. God knows that nothing short of that will really fulfill the deepest longings and yearnings of our spirit. The Good Shepherd sends fierce sheep dogs to harass us until we turn back to the fold. It's futile to ask him to call off the dogs until we change direction.

God does want us to have what we need. He taught us to pray, "Give us this day our daily bread," which Luther says includes everything that is required to satisfy our temporal needs, such as food, clothing, shelter, families, good government, good weather, true friends, peace, and health. In an affluent nation such as ours we tend to expand these needs into security and pleasure far beyond any sensible standard.

One evening a recurrent advertisement punctuated our TV program, proposing that we buy a weekend excursion to Las Vegas. The punch line was, "You need it and you deserve it." Since our Minnesota wind-chill temperature at that moment was 50 degrees below zero, it wasn't difficult to agree that we needed a breather in warm weather, and we could even conclude that we deserved it as much as our neighbors who had just left for Hawaii. If the Lord was listening in, he must have chuckled (or wept) at the nonsense of redefining our needs to include Las Vegas. But our whole culture is victimized by such distortion.

Isn't it safe to conclude that the Lord wants no part in making us wealthy, unless we use this wealth in the service of others, or that he deplores our gaining office or power unless we use such influence for the welfare of all? God's only interest in our attaining wealth or power is what effect, for good or ill, it might have on us. If possessions tend to make us proud and self-indulgent, we could expect him to take them away.

Probably our whole way of life has to be measured by spiritual objectives. If it's harder for God to bring us around to his way with jets and computers, he might favor our going back to donkeys and the abacus.

It takes unusual grace to believe that when something goes wrong with our plans, it might be that God is administering his kind of comfort. Speaking of adversities, the writer in Hebrews tells us, "God is treating you as sons; for what son is there whom his father does not discipline. . . . For the moment all discipline seems painful rather than pleasant; later it yields the peaceful fruit of righteousness to those who have been trained by it."

Most of us will not take this counsel as literally as the old missionary who, upon getting sick, was cheered that God had not forgotten him but was now spanking him a little. It would be folly to conclude that every time we run into adversity—sickness, loss of a job, collapse of investments, election defeat, rejection, the death of a loved one—that God is spanking us. He suffers with us. But if we will let him, he can use adversities to good ends for us. They can prod us to reexamine what is important, and help us to shift our priorities. God has done it again and again.

When we lost our son at 24, we realized that for 25

years our family had suffered no major hurts. Suddenly we became aware of our many friends who were also burdened with tragedies. It was as if we were no longer set apart as "special," but had become part of the human family where misfortunes and sorrows are built into life. Grief-stricken as we were, this thought brought strange comfort. Our prayers for his safety had not been answered, but something good was emerging for us.

The worst thing that can happen to us is that we can go on blithely in our preoccupation with self, relatively untouched by reversals, growing complacent, a bit proud, and quite indifferent to the suffering world. God has little chance to reach us, because we will not cry to him. We may even forget to thank him.

If he doesn't specifically arrange our adversities, he may indeed allow them to happen—for our own good, and for our eventual comfort.

When Doubts Torment You

You doubt that which you most want to believe. Your child is very sick. The doctor says she'll get well, but you worry. What if the doctor is wrong? Doubts keep welling up, and they don't subside until your child is back home, safe and sound. A man may have no reason to doubt that his sweetheart loves him, but he may worry about it, simply because losing her love would shatter his life. You doubt that which you most want to believe.

No one doubts that which can easily be proven, such

as four plus four equals eight, or Napoleon once ruled France, or the Missouri flows into the Mississippi.

It's in the field of religious beliefs that doubts are most harassing, because faith in God is ultimately the basis for faith in almost anything else—other people, the future, even oneself. If there is no God, what is there to count on? People don't worry much about whether there is a God until they very much want a God. They don't bother with whether Jesus is the Son of God who forgives sins unless they feel the burden of guilt and sin.

In the New Testament we meet the apostle Thomas, often dubbed "the doubter." Jesus appeared to the other disciples after the resurrection, but Thomas was absent. Told that they had seen Jesus, Thomas in anguish said he could not believe unless he could touch Jesus's hands and side. He doubted, precisely because he wanted more than anything else to have the Lord be alive.

When Jesus did show up to Thomas, he chided him, "Have you believed because you have seen me? Blessed are those who have not seen and yet believe." That's you and me, and the whole human race, ever since the Lord's ascension. Like Thomas, we may be plagued by doubts. Given no vision in the sky, we are summoned still to believe. And deep down, we want to believe.

A philosopher has said, "The promise is so vast that a feeling of incredulity will creep in." And what a promise the biblical story holds! Back away from it for a moment, and look at it as for the first time.

We say that the God who created and manages this vast

universe decided to colonize a tiny island, earth, with his family, his sons and daughters. And, that when his children turned from him and were imprisoned by the enemy, instead of abandoning them, God came to earth in the person of Jesus, God the Son, to win them back—at the fantastic price of giving his life on a cross. We go on to say that this God gives each of us an open line to him. We can dial him direct, and the line is never busy—he hears our most trivial prayer. And when death is done with us, God puts us on our feet again in a more wonderful part of his empire to live with him forever.

Is there any other story in all the world to so tax our imaginations? How can modest people believe they are important to God? Doubt seems more reasonable (and humble) than faith.

But to doubt leaves us on an uncharted sea without a rudder. If the story is not true, then what? What is my importance in this universe if I'm not a child of God but merely a blob of protoplasm? Is the universe itself any more than a cold, impersonal, and cruel machine, if there is no God? Is there any reason to struggle for justice and mercy and righteousness?

The option of doubt is really too frightening to entertain. An empty heaven, no judge on the bench, no Savior to forgive, no good Father waiting for us. In *Pippa Passes,* Browning says, "This Christianity, it may be so or it may not be so, but will you have it be so if it can?" We answer that, more than anything else in all the world we want it to be so, all doubts notwithstanding.

Faith is stronger than doubt, because it attaches itself to the truth. Doubt is wedded to an ultimate lie. And God has other ways than a laboratory or a computer to give us his own kind of "proof." We are not left to wishful thinking alone. We do not create God in our image. We are created in his, and he has provided us with built-in connections to him. "Deep calls to deep," says the psalmist. And Paul says that God's Spirit witnesses with our spirit that we are children of his. There is a profound intuition in the human spirit that will not settle for a harsh, impersonal, and indifferent universe.

Robert Ingersoll, a late 19th-century agnostic, said at his brother's grave:

> Life is but a narrow vale between the cold and barren peaks of two eternities. We strive in vain to look beyond the heights. We cry aloud and the only answer is the echo of our wailing cry. From the voiceless lips of the unreplying dead there comes no word, but in the night of death hope sees a star, and listening love can hear the rustle of a wing.

We have more than an echo. God has broken the silence. He has spoken to us through the prophets. He has appeared in the person of God the Son. His Spirit broods over us through Word and sacrament. And through the centuries he has provided a cradle of believing people, the church, in which doubts lose their hold, and we are caught up in a kingdom, at once mysterious and real, where we find the key to life.

When You Think You're a Failure

By God's standards we are all failures. There's none really good, says the psalmist. By God's incredibly high measurements of love and holiness, none of us will pass.

By the world's standards, we may be successes or failures, but it may make little difference to God how we rate. God accepts us as sons and daughters and sweeps us into his kingdom of love, no matter how well or ill we score. We belong to him and can afford to fail.

But we will be troubled by worldly standards, many of

them trivial, some of them fraudulent. Money, for instance. What was his top salary? How much of an estate did he leave? It was said of Abraham Lincoln, who died poor, "He forgot to collect his earnings."

In our rapidly changing society, some people lose their jobs at 50 and have to start over again. It's a crushing experience. Why hadn't he climbed high enough on the ladder to ensure his place until retirement? Unless he can remember that he was caught in the storm of economic forces over which he had little or no control (like a tornado wrecking the house he had just built), he's likely to think himself a failure.

We may set goals that almost guarantee failure. A runner who trains to run the 100 yard dash in 9.5, and does it in 9.8, has failed—because he set his goals too high. Had he set out to run the distance in 11 seconds, he would have been a great success by the goals he had set. There's nothing wrong, is there, in setting ideals too high, and reaching out for them, and failing? Jesus told us to love our neighbors as ourselves, knowing full well that we would never be able to kill our self-concerns to that degree, but that in trying we might come a long way toward the goal. We are to dream the impossible dream!

What fathers and mothers, having seen the high hopes they've had for their children shattered, haven't asked themselves where they failed? They may have failed (or maybe not), but they must remember that a child is not a piece of clay that necessarily yields to the loving and wise hand of a parent. Children are independent beings who insist on finding their own way. No one, not even a parent, can be held responsible for the failure of another.

Failure may sometimes be the closing of one door and the opening of another. In my 20 years at the seminary I have known several young men who failed in the highly competitive examinations for medical school and who turned to theology. Becoming excellent pastors, they later were convinced that they were finding greater satisfaction than they would have found in medicine.

Thousands of people can look back on failures that turned them toward opportunities of unpredictable success. It could well be that the most unfortunate are those who have never known failure. If everything has gone their way, they may become proud, condescending, and insensitive to the hurts and anxieties of others.

It is comforting to know that we have a God who wants us to set such high goals for ourselves that we must fail. Even more comforting it is that whatever our failures, whether by his standards or by the standards of the world, he loves us still, and honors us as sons and daughters in his kingdom.

When Your Marriage Is in Trouble

Marriage rests on two foundations: love and a promise. You came to love each other. Then you appeared before God and society and promised "to love her, comfort her, honor and keep her in sickness and in health, and, forsaking all others, keep only to her, so long as we both shall live." Each made the same promise to the other. Implied in that promise was another promise—that if God gave you children, together you would love them and care for them as long as you lived.

The feeling of love alone is never strong enough to keep your marriage going. Feelings are up and down— but duty is constant. You made a promise. In days when love is strained and seems to fade, duty takes over. Love itself has a chance to grow strong and mellow only when it is reinforced by promise and duty.

Every marriage runs into some rocky stretches. To give up and get off the road doesn't mean you'll end up on a smooth stretch. More than likely, you'll veer off into a jungle of pretense, remorse, and shame. Your companions from then on are the ghosts of what might have been.

It's possible to explain, perhaps even to justify, the increase of divorce rates today. But whatever the circumstances, you can't justify breaking a promise. You can't find excuses for robbing your children of love and security. Any defense you make for your right to pleasure or fulfillment will be phony. Neither God nor any code of honor will accept your defense.

These broad statements may seem harsh. A soldier may think it harsh to be told that if need be he may have to die for his country. It's equally true for a father and mother— if need be they'll have to put their own fulfillment aside for the good of the family. They may not recognize it, but such commitment is the key to fulfillment for them.

Marriage always brings together two imperfect people. Each has good qualities and each has not-so-good qualities. The romantic notion that with marriage faults disappear is nonsense. To be sure, each may help the other overcome undesirable traits, but that takes some doing. Unless they are vigilant, they may actually intensify bad qualities in each other.

If both partners defend their right to personal fulfillment (whatever fulfillment may mean), they should never have married. Service—not fulfillment—is the name of the marriage game. Fulfillment is the fairy that steals in as you go about loving and helping each other. It will elude you if you seek it. Aim at loving and serving and you'll get fulfillment thrown in. That's the way God designed life, and you can't cheat the architect.

Nothing frightens me as much as today's increase in divorce, because it sets children adrift on a stormy sea. No matter if both separated parents assure the children of their love, the children will be haunted: "They didn't love me enough to swallow their selfishness and spare me this great pain." And the pain won't be less because there are more children today with the same pain. If the boat capsizes and you're drowning, there's no joy in knowing that others are drowning too. What ghastly price will our society pay in the future? Children in today's world are insecure enough without having their parents remove the most important prop of all.

It matters little how successful a man is in business or profession if he defaults on his highest assignment as husband and father. And it's a sorry bargain for a wife and mother to succeed as a writer or artist if on the way she has scuttled her family.

I know there is forgiveness with God for all failures. I do not forget that marvelous truth. But not even God can remove all the wreckage. "The bird with the broken pinion never flew as high again."

Whenever you think the road is rocky (and it would be strange if you never ran into such a stretch), remember that if you decide to get off the road, you'll probably find any other road worse—not only rocky, but with no road map at all.

The real comfort lies in keeping the promise, even when it means enduring temporary distress. People who have done just that can tell you there are good stretches ahead. Love itself revives and grows mellower with understanding. And your children and grandchildren will grow strong in your love.

When You Fear Growing Old

I'm frank to say that I fear growing too old. But when is too old? My uncle at 96 has diminished powers of seeing and hearing, but a sharp mind. Has he grown too old?

Fear is nothing new for me. I had anxieties and fears in high school. I certainly had them when I was responsible for my work and for my growing family. The fears of adolescence have now given way to the fears of aging. I rather think I prefer the ones I have now.

It startled me to read that of all people who have lived

to be 65 since the dawn of history, more than 25% are still alive. And our crowd is growing. Having passed three score and ten, I now have less fear of dying than of living too long. I think of languishing in a nursing home, my memory largely gone and my usefulness to anyone in serious question.

My great grandfather died at 93 and was sound of mind, my grandparents (whom I knew well) died swiftly in their 80s with no long prelude of illness, and my parents were only 66 when death struck them down. I have little family experience with lingering old age.

The four years since I officially left my desk and became classified as retired have been among the best years, if not the best. Both Nora and I are in good health. We've had the leisure to focus on each other and on our sprawling family of children and grandchildren, and on friends old and new. No longer do I have continuous, pervasive responsibility for a school or a parish.

I've been puzzled, and not a little impatient, with everybody insisting that we think about the sociobiologic issues of getting old on the one hand, and the problems of death and dying on the other. Why not just let us grow old, and when the time comes just let us die, without making it a duty to think about it too much?

This sounds naive, I realize, and almost irresponsible. Caring for and making use of the increasing number of older people certainly are inescapable issues for government, church, and industry. And I am willing to cooperate in the wisdom that may emerge from the studies. But I find myself comfortable with the tempo of the years.

Autumn has always been my favorite season, even when I was young. The drama of life begins to wind down and the stage begins to empty. Birds wing south, the sun becomes a bit lazy, and the leaves don their riotous best for their silent requiem. Nature becomes serene and calm, and invites the human spirit to join her. The winter of sleep is near, but winter itself we know is but an interlude. The poet's question, "If winter comes, can spring be far behind?" is a promise.

No doubt I have been conditioned to old age by my grandfather, who in many ways was my companion from the time I can remember until I left for college. I never saw him work. I see him still, with a book and pipe, in the summer shade under the elm, or on the porch, or ambling up to the mailbox with his cane well before the mail arrived. I'm fascinated again by the memory of his accounts of the pioneer days and of his boyhood in Norway. I can never remember him saying a harsh or cynical word. For me he was the symbol of wisdom, strength, piety, compassion—even humor. If this was what growing old could mean, why shouldn't a boy long for that day?

I try not to fight against the ebbing strength, nor protest the aches and pains of worn parts that have done good work. I'm glad for the medical repairs to keep them going a bit longer. Why should I have the lusty appetite of 30, or the ready sex, or the muscles tingling for a race with my grandchildren? "Grandpa, remember your age!" I'm told that brain cells do not give up so quickly, and I'm glad.

A friend of mine, a program director in a large hospital, told me, "Al, we've made an idolatry of life." He believes there's something basically wrong, and certainly counterproductive for happiness, with our almost pathological eagerness to outmaneuver death. I was struck with the truth of his observation one evening when a group of us older friends had been visiting. Suddenly I realized that for an hour we had been talking about nothing but diets, exercise, calories, cholesterol, pills, insomnia, and surgeons. We hadn't yet come to morticians. Evidently we were counting on escaping them.

Death is in the offing. There's nothing new about that. If we have allowed each day to bring its opportunities for service and joy (and a bit of pain), with minimum concern for the next day's menu, and if we have not lost sight of our Lord's promise that the next chapter of life will be immeasurably more wonderful than this one, we can enjoy being carried along on the stream of life, and take pleasure in the silent flow of time, making merry with the fellow passengers God gives us.

When You
Feel You Have
Lost
God

Read the Bible from cover to cover, and you won't find
God asking you to feel one thing or another. He has much
to say about what you do, but not about how you feel.
You may have lost God, but not because you *feel* you have.

Feelings are capricious. You have little control over
them. You do have something to say about what you will
to do and about what you will to believe. But even when
you believe the truth and do the good, you still may feel
down. Don't worry about it.

A lot of fine people have been sent reeling down an unhappy road because someone told them that they ought to *feel* something to find favor with God. Someone asks, "Haven't you had the feeling that God is near?" or "When did you first feel that God had forgiven your sins?" or "When did you first feel that you loved all people?" or "When did you really feel that you had come to Christ?" Implied in each of these questions is that at some high point you should have had an overwhelming feeling about God. And maybe you haven't had it.

I like what Jesus told his followers: "If any man's will is to do his will, he shall know whether the teaching is from God or whether I am speaking on my own authority." If you are to *know* and to *feel,* you'll have to experiment by *doing* his will. In no way can you sit back and meditate or study and hope either to know the truth about God or to feel anything about God. You have to plunge into doing God's will, despite all your doubts and all your uneasy feelings.

We can't dictate to God what kind of feelings he should give us. And there's something very sad about people who run from one church to another, hoping to get some kind of feeling. If they think they have found the right feeling with one group, often they reject Christian brothers and sisters—even family members—in another group.

God gives assurance in his own time and in his own way. He gives feelings too, but we can't dictate to him what kind of feelings he should give us. His test is neither in assurance nor in feelings. Jesus made that clear when he said, "Whoever does the will of God is my brother, and sister, and mother."

Unfortunately, in our day we have concentrated on feelings, often in a disastrous way. A moving picture marquee had the slogan, "If it feels good, it's OK." What nonsense. If it feels good to murder, it's OK. If it feels good to commit adultery, it's OK. If it feels good to get another spouse, it's OK.

You can't trust your feelings, even about God. For nearly 2000 years the people who have taken Christ seriously have had something to tell you about God and the Bible. You had better trust them instead of your feelings. If you don't, you'll be on a roller coaster, up and down, and you'll have no comfort at all.

Go back to the wonderful message of the Bible. It tells you that God created you, redeemed you, and claims you as his own, no matter what you think or how you feel. Fasten yourself to that promise, and don't let it go. He will give you the feelings you may need. Do his will, as you discover it, and let your feelings fall where they may.

When You Question Your Spiritual Growth

All through nature we see growth. Plants grow and children grow. Astronomers say the universe itself is growing.

People who take their Christian faith seriously like some assurance that across the years they have grown in faith and hope and love.

Growth in the Spirit is not always easy to measure. In fact, spirituality itself is difficult to define. Is it an ecstasy of feeling? Is it essentially a moral quality? Is it awareness of God's presence?

Also, if you are growing spiritually, do you know it? Do others? And if you do grow, do you move on gradually or in spurts?

I have now lived more than 70 years. Am I farther along now in my life with God (in my spirituality) than when I was eight or twelve? Do I have a greater childlike trust in God now than I did 60 years ago?

I have never felt a more sublime faith than the night my father was hovering between life and death in the next bedroom. I was 13, the oldest of six children. Full of fear, I crept into bed with mother and asked her what we would do if father were to die. I still remember her stroking my forehead and saying, "God will take care of us." I fell asleep cradled in a great love and care. I don't think I have ever quite reached that point since.

Do I have a more selfless spirit? I'm not sure. Certainly at 13 I never bothered to protect myself against the uncertainties of the future. It could be that now, with a few aches and pains that age brings on, I turn in on myself more than I did then.

Is my commitment to God stronger? I remember a striking moment in my senior year at college. It was spring and the sun was bright. I was sitting alone on the lawn in front of Old Main. Word had just come to me that I would be giving the valedictory for the class. Suddenly a sense of joy and gratitude swept through me. God had been enormously good to let me finish college, and I owed my life to him. That moment of commitment has never again come in quite that way. Was this the high moment of growth for me? Have I been on a plateau, or have I been slipping, ever since?

How about my level of hope? That ought to be one measure. I rather suspect that this has been eroding across the years. It's harder for me to hope now than when I was 20 or 30. I'm not talking about hope in life after death, but about hope for life on earth for my grandchildren. I have fears I never had 40 years ago.

The Scriptures do speak of our going from strength to strength. They speak of "mounting up on wings as eagles," of being renewed in the image of God, of growing more and more Christ-like. Growth should be our aim and hope.

But at best, to try to measure how we're doing has difficulties. It is easy for a person who has overcome drugs and alcoholism to chalk this up as gain, or for a person who was indifferent to church and worship who now hungers for the Word and for fellowship, or for a person who has overcome a passion for security and has begun to freely give money for the welfare of others. These gains are measurable, but the inner growth of the Spirit is not that easy to chart.

If God should grade us like a teacher to determine when we would qualify for his kingdom, where would we be? When would we have peace? He knows the path of our progress, surely, or our regress. But what does he do about it?

In one sense, he does nothing. We are his, accepted by him, simply because he created us and redeemed us to be

Valley Forge
gets collection

By **LINDA LLOYD**
ght-Ridder Newspapers
LLEY FORGE, Pa. —

nearly 20 years,
ge C. Neumann has
ed the country,
ting Revolutionary
weapons and
rabilia, and storing
in his Durham,
farmhouse.

Neumann's passion
e colonial weaponry
so did his collection,
muskets, rifles,
s, cannons and a host
her military ac-
ies worth a total of
0 to $750,000.

reflection grew so
in fact, that it
owed Neumann's
ent and attic and
the history buff and
essman to worry
its security.

Now his worries are
ended.

The National Park
Service, aided by a $350,000
donation from Sun Co. in
Radnor, Pa., announced its
purchase for $640,000 of the
Neumann collection.

The entire collection —
80 muskets and rifles, 350
swords, 115 pole arms
(spears), 220 bayonets,
axes and knives plus 700
accoutrements including
powder horns, cartridges
and canteens — can be
seen by the public from
Dec. 19 to Dec. 24 at the
park visitor center.

his. We may reject him, but he never rejects us, whether we grow or slip.

The Sacrament of Holy Baptism is just this kind of assurance. We became his then, as spiritual babes. We became one of his family, heirs of his kingdom. We've been living in that Baptism ever since.

I know of nothing in all Scripture to compare with this towering truth to give us comfort. I don't have to feed my life into a computer to discover how I stand with him.

Of course, I hope that these 70 years have not been barren, that the years have not brought regression. But I leave the measuring to him. If I have grown these 60-70 years, fine. I hope I have. If I've been slipping—he claims me still!

When Grace Seems Too Easy

You tell me that the Christian faith doesn't appeal to you because it's too easy. Your preacher talks about God being so gracious that he lets you off. What's happened to his demands, or doesn't he really have any? If he has some, doesn't he enforce them? Even the Rotary Club makes you attend meetings. If you miss, you have to make it up.

You say you feel that you're not taken seriously. What kind of God doesn't seem to care what you do, as long as you depend on him to see you through? This whole matter of grace, and grace alone, has you baffled. It seems too easy to be true.

You raise some disturbing questions. The apostle Paul admitted that this whole matter of God's grace would seem an offense, a stumbling block, sheer foolishness.

I'm reminded of what John Steinbeck observed in his delightful book, *Travels with Charlie.* He had drifted into a little country church in Vermont on a Sunday morning. Here are his reactions:

> The service did my heart and I hope my soul some good. It is our practise now, at least in the large cities, to find from our psychiatric priesthood that our sins aren't really sins at all but accidents that are set in motion by forces beyond our control. There was no such nonsense in this church. . . .For some years now God has been a pal to us, practising togetherness, and that causes the same emptiness a father does playing softball with his son. But this Vermont God cared enough about me to go to a lot of trouble kicking the hell out of me. He put my sins in a new perspective. Whereas they had been small and mean and nasty and best forgotten, this minister gave them some size and bloom and dignity. I hadn't been thinking very well of myself for some years, but if my sins had this dimension there was some pride left. I wasn't a naughty child but a first rate sinner, and I was going to catch it. . . . I felt so revived in spirit that I put five dollars in the plate.

Far from minimizing the importance of our sins (or making light of God's laws), the Christian message that, through God's mercy, a person is justified or made right, takes our wrongdoing with terrifying seriousness. Your best performance won't set things right. It took the life and death and resurrection of God the Son, Jesus Christ, to meet the demands of the exalted requirements that God makes for you and me.

It could be that God's way of grace seems too bland, too soothing, too easy—because we have not seriously tried meeting the demands of God's law. Have you tried to love the Lord with all your heart, and your neighbor as yourself? Have you tried to do to others what you would they should do to you? And how about righteousness, purity of heart, the forgiving spirit—have you been striving for these goals?

Paul did, and Luther did—with an intensity that finally drove them to the wall. The demands of God became a towering mountain impossible to scale. They had no alternative but to give up. If they were to live with God, or even decently with themselves, they had to find another way. They had to throw themselves on the sheer mercy of God.

Most of us have never given God's demands this kind of try. We've tended to tailor his demands to our capacities or to society's expectations, so we've escaped both the fury of his law and the glory of his grace.

Our difficulties with grace may mean that we come to the second chapter of the book before reading the first. In the first chapter a man tries every which way to keep his business afloat, but he fails utterly and collapses into bankruptcy. It's in the second chapter that his friend comes along, pays his bills, and gives him new capital to start afresh.

Because we don't take seriously God's fierce demands for holiness and mercy and love and purity and honesty and selflessness, we fail to understand that we are bankrupt before him. And if you think you have reasonably good credit, what's so great about your friend investing money in you? What's so wonderful about God's grace, if you believe you have the investments of a fairly decent life to fall back on?

We face two courts. The first is the society in which we live. It's fairly easy to get a good verdict here (and a nice obituary) by simply being a decent citizen. The second court is the supreme court, the high tribunal of God, where even the secret motives of the heart come under sentence. The psalmist cried, "If thou, O Lord, shouldst mark iniquities, O Lord, who could stand?" Here not only the evil we have done comes under survey, but in addition the massive amount of good we might have done but neglected. In this court you won't ask for justice. You'll have but one cry, "God be merciful to me."

Here grace enters the picture. The God who sits on the bench is the same God who died on a cross to rescue us from the court's condemnation.

You may well ask, "If I have never stood terrified before God's high court, can I find any comfort at the foot of the cross? If the court is not real for me, will grace ever seem real?"

And still another question, "If I find myself at the foot of the cross, am I never again to be troubled by the court?"

Yes and no. Until you die, you are two people. You are the old Adam, bad and selfish, but you are also new in Christ. You shift from one self to the other. The bad you ought to stand terrified before the court. The new you should revel in the freedom and forgiveness of the cross.

If the terror of the court fades away and you forget all about it, the wonder of the cross may fade too. Your life is like a teeter-totter; the lower one end is down, the higher the other. The more bankrupt your own efforts to obey God's high law, the greater the glory of his having done it for you. If you've taken God out of the courtroom, you'll probably not find him at the cross either.

Nor is the new you done with God's demands. They exist no longer as a brief in the courtroom, but they're still there—as a guide along the road with God. The new you seeks ways to thank God for grace by doing precisely those things that earlier tormented you as law.

When you complain that grace seems too soothing and bland, you're really complaining that our whole society, including the church, has taken the courtroom too casually. We have allowed the high bench to be empty—no judge in sight. And if we're not even important enough to be judged, we're in deep trouble. Steinbeck was right. In the courtroom we feel important again.

If you're important enough to send to hell, you're important enough to be rescued for heaven. This is what grace is all about.

When You Don't Feel Religious

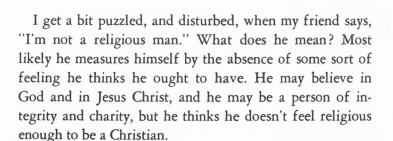

I get a bit puzzled, and disturbed, when my friend says, "I'm not a religious man." What does he mean? Most likely he measures himself by the absence of some sort of feeling he thinks he ought to have. He may believe in God and in Jesus Christ, and he may be a person of integrity and charity, but he thinks he doesn't feel religious enough to be a Christian.

Nor is his situation made easier by the current fashion of people telling others about the high moment when they became Christian, even implying that they've since been riding some cloud of untroubled peace and joy. So my friend goes his troubled way, thinking that if he can't match the emotional ecstasy of well-publicized born-again people, he's outside of the family of God.

I admit that I have mixed feelings when someone "witnesses" to some remarkable experience he's had with God. On one hand, I am encouraged by his new enthusiasm and ardor, and a bit envious. On the other hand, I'm haunted by the uneasy feeling that, to be a full-fledged Christian, I ought to be able to match his ardor, and usually I can't. So should I run around looking for some "experience?"

I take encouragement from the apostle Paul. Who can match his experience on the Damascus road? He was struck blind by a blazing light. He heard the voice of Jesus. But he hardly ever mentions this to anyone. In the New Testament record, he refers to this remarkable moment only twice. Even then, he talks about it in guarded language: "God was pleased to reveal his Son to me, in order that I might preach him among the Gentiles."

Paul must have known that if he dwelt on his particular experience, he might mislead people into thinking that they would have to have a similar experience if they were to be followers of Jesus.

Don't get me wrong. A life with God will generate feelings far more profoundly than a symphony or sunset or the words of a loved one. But our Lord was far more concerned about moving the wills of people than moving their feelings.

If you help your grumbling neighbor when you don't feel like doing it at all, if you are patient and uncomplaining when you feel like blowing your stack, if you come to church to thank God when you feel depressed and dejected—in short, when you defy your feelings and do what you think is right—you're probably much more "religious" than if you were to wait for some celestial feeling to overcome you and sweep you into action. We have little control over our feelings. We have more control over our wills.

Moreover, how do you measure the intensity of a feeling? Let us say that two men fall in love with two women. One man is exuberant. He tells everyone about his love. The other is restrained. He tells no one. He has trouble telling even her. Are we to conclude that the noisier one has the deeper feelings and will be the more devoted husband?

My mother was quiet and humble. I doubt that I've known anyone more devout. She always felt a bit uncomfortable in the "witnessing" groups, and I think she lived with some uneasiness that she couldn't be loquacious about her Lord. But it wasn't necessary for her to expose her feelings for us. We knew how deep they were. Her life was an eloquent revelation. In spite of this, she may have gone to her grave wondering if she was "religious" enough.

Most people who have a striking spiritual experience will face two dangers. First, they may always refer back to this one instance for validation, and forget about the hard, sometimes uninspiring life of the disciple. Second, they may leave their Lord altogether if they fail to experience repeated high moments. They forget that they have no right to dictate to the Lord what feelings he should give them.

I remember a wonderful, devout woman dying from cancer. Two days before her death, her daughters came to me and told me their mother was in deep distress because she didn't think she was good enough to have God accept her, though they had assured her that she was the best of mothers. I went to see her. She poured out her heart to me. She said, "Not only am I not good enough, but I have deceived my daughters into thinking I'm better than I am." It didn't take her long to remember that her status with God depended neither on how well she had done nor how dedicated she felt, but on the simple, great truth that Jesus Christ had died to make up for all her failings, both in doing and in feeling.

If you are among those who say, "I'm not religious," please take stock of what criteria you're using. Are you depending on your feelings to qualify you? Are you under the impression that your life must be faultless before you can approach God? In either instance, don't read yourself out of God's family.

You have a right to come to God in boldness. Rely on his promises, that he receives you as you are (because Christ has opened the door for you), and push on into the kingdom to claim the comforts and joys and duties that await you.

When the Bible Puzzles You

There's no book in all the world's literature that has so profoundly shaped our lives as the Bible. It's not one book, really. It's a library of 66 books, some perhaps 5000 years old. Not until A.D. 400 were the last books, the New Testament's 27 manuscripts, accepted into one collection.

We call it God's book, the Word of God. Obviously it was not published in heaven and dropped down by angels. It is a record of what has transpired in the lives of people who took God seriously. Through its many literary forms —history, parable, drama, poetry—we believe that God reveals himself to us and comes to us.

It has not been easy to escape two extremes in dealing with the Bible—on one hand, to think of it as virtually having dropped down from heaven, with every word and comma in perfect order, and on the other hand, to put it in the same class with all great, inspirational literature. Neither extreme satisfies the believer.

To regard the Bible as perfect, correct even in all its historical and scientific allusions, puts the believer on an endless chase to defend it against historical and scientific research. To think of it as just another great book among others is to rob us of its divine revelation and authority.

Even if we want to regard the Bible as perfect, we do not go to it to learn about the shape of the earth (Christians did this in the day of Galileo and Copernicus), to discover skills in medicine, or to ferret out the secret of the atom. God has other ways of letting us in on telephones, penicillin, and computers. But God has no book but the Bible to reveal himself as a God of infinite love. This is the Bible's purpose.

If we remember this, there will still be puzzling questions. How could God destroy the earth in Noah's flood? How could he approve or even order the genocide of whole peoples to protect the Israelites? How could he allow a good man, Job, to be the victim of one unjust tragedy after another?

If you are to find comfort in the Bible, you'll have to

put these questions on the shelf and turn to the dominant motifs of the book. Don't start with Genesis, but with the Gospels. Go first to God the Son, who in his love for humanity gave his life on a cross for us. This may puzzle you even more. How can God love you that much?

But this is a comforting mystery, one that captures you for a life of meaning and mercy. With your eye on Jesus, you learn of God as a great and good father who hears the prayers of his children, guards them from evil, forgives their sins, and has a heavenly home prepared for them when death is done with them.

A God who punishes may be less puzzling than a God who forgives. All human beings know they deserve punishment. This is the way of simple justice. But to be caught up in a mercy that sweeps all our wretchedness away, to be received as if we had never sinned—can this be true?

This is the puzzle to end all puzzles. It is the truth to tower above all truths. It is the comfort to dwarf all other comforts.

When Rumors Distress You

How disturbed should you be by rumors? That depends on whether the rumor damages you or someone else. If someone else is being hurt, it is your clear duty to do something to stop the rumor's spread. If it's a threat to you alone, there may be better ways to deal with it than becoming distressed and striking back.

I've known people who go to the defense of others and hardly ever bother to defend themselves. They take almost literally the Lord's counsel, "If any one strikes you on the right cheek, turn to him the other also." They do this out of strength, not weakness.

But rumors and gossip are damaging. They grow like cancer. What began as a small lie soon becomes bloated into a big one. It is but common sense to nip it in the bud—without vindictiveness and with concern for all, even for whomever started it.

I remember as a boy being the victim of a rumor. A village storekeeper told someone I had lifted something from his shelves. The rumor reached my father. He asked me if it was true. When I said no, he marched me at once into the store and had the storekeeper apologize to me. I don't remember being especially upset by the rumor, but I do remember how gratifying it was to have my father trust me and come to my defense.

Whenever the gossip about you is untrue, you have the comfort of knowing that your integrity is not at stake. You are in the clear. Even so, the talk may be hurting someone dear to you. A husband, for instance, charged falsely with infidelity, may need to guard his wife and family from anguish by squelching the rumor.

It is a sad commentary on human nature that most of us tend to enjoy hearing something bad about people. We have a hard time resisting the urge to pass on the wretched tidbit to others. We say, "I don't know whether it's true, but have you heard. . . ?"

Nor is it uncommon even for the press to take a rumor and pass it on with introductions such as "It is alleged," "It is rumored," or "It is reported from an unconfirmed source." More than likely, what follows is not some eulogy to a person's goodness.

We must guard ourselves therefore from cynicism and disillusionment when we become victims of rumor. This is par for the course in a fallen world such as ours, inhabited by people such as we.

There are three courses to follow to reduce the damage of rumor.

First, be vigilant that you neither begin one nor repeat one. In commenting on the eighth commandment, "Thou shalt not bear false witness against thy neighbor," Luther gives this counsel: "That we do not backbite or slander our neighbor, but apologize for him, speak well of him, and put the most charitable construction on all that he does."

Second, come to the defense of anyone who is victimized by gossip.

Third, if you are the victim, remind yourself of two things. You have no guilt because you did no wrong. This in itself is profound comfort. Then, remember that truth tends to create its own defense, and that the innocent one is often vindicated by history. Truth will out. You may not need to bother to defend truth or yourself.

Best of all, you can face God with a good conscience.

When You Wonder if Your Life Has Counted

With advancing years, people often look back and wonder if their lives have added up to anything significant. Is the world any better for their having lived? Couldn't the world have gotten along very well without them?

Alfred B. Nobel discovered dynamite a century ago. If today he could assess his amazing discovery, would he be able to balance off the good dynamite has done (in mining, for instance) against the bombs that have killed hundreds of thousands? Every advance in science presents us with this dilemma. Would even Orville and Wilbur Wright, who set the stage for air travel at Kitty Hawk in 1903, wonder if they might better have left us with the less hectic tempo of trains and ships?

Few of us have dramatically altered the shape of life by what we have done. We've been able to accumulate money, for instance, or doubled the size of the farm. Has this done more good, or less, for us and for those who came after us?

Everybody can put some things in the credit column. You did do some good things, after all. But the moment you begin to count the good you might have done, but didn't, and put this list in the debit column, you're uneasy. You'd like to forget all about striking any kind of balance.

But most of us cannot forget. Memories haunt us. Someone counted on us, and we didn't come through. We were too busy, or we were afraid to get involved. In Jesus' familiar parable of the Good Samaritan, one wonders how the priest and the Levite came to terms with the memory of having left the poor man in the ditch. Our lives may be littered by such missed opportunities.

Quite apart from specific instance, every father will wonder if he was a good father. Every mother will wonder if she was a good mother. Even if the verdict of their children is an unconditional yes, they'll still wonder.

A friend of mine, an able surgeon, expressed his misgivings about what he was doing. He said, "I'm but a high-grade plumber. I cut and stitch and patch, and give them a chance to live again. But I have nothing to do with why they should live. Why should they live?"

I had no easy answer. After all, is the goal of life simply to keep our hearts beating and our feet walking? Our almost pathetic preoccupation with health care may be a symptom of having no answer. Is it a triumph to fill our nursing homes with people who no longer recognize even their children?

Once we search for a bigger answer than simply to live, eat, and sleep well, to continue life to another generation, to work and play, we are on the trail of the meaning of life itself. Why should anything exist at all?

Nor will it be enough to say that we live in order to have more pleasure than pain, more happiness than sorrow. If that were the answer, the whole of existence could be a huge blunder. An impartial judge would say that throughout humanity's long history, the cargo of pain far outweighs the fleeting moments of pleasure. Even in our age, when we obviously have adequate food and shelter, how do we measure the loneliness, the fears, the frustrations, the shame, the regrets that burden great numbers of people?

The church founders had an answer: *The measure of life is to glorify God and to serve him and to enjoy him forever.* Whether you are rich or poor, learned or unlearned, powerful or dispossessed, whether you've known mostly sorrow or mostly joy, your life has great and ultimate meaning if it is nestled in God and in doing his will.

Someone will protest, "That's a religious answer, and

doesn't come to terms with the hard stuff of sickness and poverty and failure, or even with what happens to the world." Yes, it does seem to shift the scene from survival of corporations and nations, from the size of your farm, from the promotions you've had, from the estate you may leave your children.

This answer reminds you that you are an eternal being, with a short tenure on this planet. You are a citizen of an imperishable kingdom. And your life will be measured by the standards of that kingdom. These standards call for love and honesty and mercy, whether they produce immediate prosperity and happiness or pain and sorrow. The goal is no longer security or survival. The goal is service. He is greatest who serves, said Jesus.

Instinctively, every person knows there's greater joy in giving service than in receiving service. "It is more blessed to give than to receive," said Jesus. My friend had discovered this. He said, "It's more fun to write a check than to get one. It's more fun to distribute than to accumulate." A great executive will look back with more joy on those instances when he has helped someone in need, encouraged someone whose courage was flagging, allayed the grief of someone who was weeping, than on the success of his corporation.

Of course, even if we shift our standards to those of the kingdom, our balances may still be in trouble. Did we give more comfort than pain? In this competitive world, did we crush more people than we encouraged? Were we compassionate or indifferent? Will we have left the world a better place for having lived? What will be the verdict of an all-knowing God?

It is at this point that the deep truths of our Christian faith come to our rescue. God alone can balance the debits and credits of our lives, and he does not even bother to see the ledger. We are his sons and daughters, ledgers or no ledgers. He loves us, no matter what. He created us in love, he redeemed us in love, he claims us in love. This is the word that comes from that cross on Golgotha nearly 2000 years ago.

God hopes that we may not be lost in the jungle of bigger businesses and farms, bigger gross national products, bigger salaries, bigger wardrobes, bigger offices, bigger cars and boats. He knows (and so do we, really) that happiness and security do not lie there. Certainly the worth of a life does not lie there.

God weeps when we leave him and are lost to him in the jungle. He hopes that we will never lose sight of the kind word, the gentle encouragement, the warm sympathy, the helping hand, the healing forgiveness. These are the stuff of our humanity, the touch of the divine on earth, the key to the joys of heaven itself.

In the vast economy of God's empire, one kind deed, one effort for justice and mercy, can never be lost. These count for eternity.

When Your Children Rebel

When young people hurt, they rebel, or at least seem to rebel. We, their parents and elders, have a hard time understanding why. Why, when we provide them with everything they need? We give them food and shelter, schooling, time for pleasure. What else do they want, or need?

Rebellion in youth is nothing new. Every generation has to find its way to selfhood and independence. Their creator gave them that right. On the way they have to defy us. They dare not have their will swallowed up by ours. They would become zombies, puppets.

But has there ever been such defiance as today? Has any generation of youth so lashed out against the normal restrictions and standards of society?

Before giving an easy yes to that question, I go back to my own youth in a small South Dakota village. We had the shelter of good homes, but we dug a cave in a hillside for our private club, out of bounds to our elders. We rolled crushed cigar stubs into newspapers and smoked clandestine cigarettes. We sneaked off to barn dances. On Halloween night we drove the town constable to distraction by tipping over every privy in the village. We paired off as couples, crowded into some father's Ford, and did our petty petting on dark country roads. I remember vividly the night my father met me at the door (about 10 P.M., I suppose) and asked, "Do you think your home is just a place to eat and sleep?" I was furious to think that he did not trust me to make my own decisions.

That was more than 50 years ago. Our rebellions were within a well-ordered and supportive world, with parents, grandparents, uncles and aunts hovering around. We grew up with the strength of the tribe. If anyone were to attack me, he'd have to take on all my uncles and aunts. Families were secure; if any man had divorced his wife in our town he would have had to leave. I had bleachers all around me, filled not only with family but with all the grown-ups in the township, cheering me on when I did well and groaning when I failed.

All sorts of young people today run the race with only silence from the bleachers. It's a lonely race. Grandparents are a thousand miles away, uncles and aunts scattered to both coasts and overseas, parents often busy with double jobs, harried by their own affluence, or casualties of the divorce courts.

Nor was it the village alone that seemed safe in my youth. The world itself seemed secure. When my son, at the age of 14, asked me what chance he and his friends had of living out a normal lifetime, I was stunned into silence. I would never have asked that at the age of 14. But that was before the bomb, before the clamorous voices predicting catastrophes of overpopulation, world hunger, and exhaustion of energy. I suddenly realized that his was a different world. His hurt was far deeper than the normal frustrations of growing up.

Is it any wonder that with their hurts they run, and don't know where to run? In a world growing increasingly unsafe, where can they find refuge? The police courts, the half-way houses, and the gangs are hardly the bleachers they need.

If there ever was a time when society needed parents who, for the sake of their children, would forget about their own self-fulfillment and look to the higher claims of their children's right to love and safety, it is now. Now, when the world of uncles and aunts and grandparents is largely gone. If God is to reach children with the comfort they so desperately need, parents will have to be his agents. All our YMCAs and YWCAs, all our schools, all our community clubs, even our churches cannot possibly fill the bleachers reserved for parents.

When young people cry "The future is now," and plunge into a bewildering maize of experience, let us listen. Isn't this the cry of someone who would like to dream of a promising tomorrow, who would like to find a solid road of abiding values, who more than anything else wants to find something worth giving a lifetime to?

And the tragedy is that they so seldom find this in us, their elders. If they have been brought up in the church and stirred by the magnetic figure of Jesus, with his call for followers who will serve their world, they often are disillusioned by the pursuit of wealth and prestige and comfort and pleasure they see in their parents and in others who sit smug and indifferent in the pews. It is we, their elders, who rob them of the dream, the tried road, the treasure worth giving up everything to have. If we listen well, it may not be the voice of rebellion we hear, but the voice of the judge indicting and sentencing us.

I cannot escape the conviction that the church is the only place where the lonely and tortured children of this uneasy age can find their bearings. Here, again and again, over and over, they are given the good news of a God who cares. Even a father and mother may forget their child, says the psalmist, but not this great and good God. I remember the story of the poor, orphaned boy who was taunted for his faith in God by someone saying, "It seems God has forgotten you," and his replying, "God hasn't forgotten, but the people he sent to care for me have forgotten." Increasingly congregations are realizing that they have been sent to listen, to try to understand, to dispel loneliness, to heal wounds, and to reach out the hand of kindness instead of raising the voice of judgment.

But it takes unusual insight, patience, and love to understand. When, to escape their loneliness, they form tight gangs, when they seek refuge in sporadic sex or living together without marriage, when in desperation they take to drugs, can we understand that they are in panic to find the dream? Or that, when apprehended for shoplifting, they are imitating their elders' mad appetite for things?

It may seem more responsible for us to come down hard on their defections, and to use the harsh instruments of authority, law, and order, to quell their rebellion. Are we not God's agents for discipline? Indeed we are. And if we discipline in love, they will understand. But without love, our efforts will but breed more rebellion.

We can take our clue from him who loved to the uttermost, to a cross.

> I did not come to judge the world but to save the world (John 12:47).

> Judge not, that you be not judged. . . . First take the log out of your own eye, and then you will see clearly to take the speck out of your brother's eye (Matt. 7:1, 5).

Jane Addams, the founder of Chicago's famous Hull House, tells of an instance in her childhood that shaped her life. She had lied to her father, a stern Dutch Calvinist, and after days of tortured conscience, she came to him with her confession of wrong. He picked her up in his arms and said, "Jane, remember that whatever you do, I will always love you." The contagion of this love, a love like that of God, drove Jane to found the great refuge for people whose lives were in shambles.

There is no healing for loneliness, fear, and failure to equal this kind of love. Since Jesus brought it into a troubled world almost 2000 years ago, it has given hope and meaning to hundreds of millions of lives. It still brings that hope!

When
Your Church
Fails You

If you're unhappy with your church, you'll find little comfort in shopping around for a church that will never fail you. And you'll find no comfort at all in giving up on all churches. You can hardly expect to keep your flame of faith glowing if you go it alone, drawing no warmth from others.

Churches do fail. For one reason or another, most congregations have an occasional bleak stretch. But unless the gospel itself has been lost, a dry period in the life of a church may set the stage for a fresh burst of the Spirit. It would be a pity to abandon the journey just as the road leads over the crest of the hill to new and exciting vistas.

The church of Jesus Christ, with its many denominations, has a vast variety of forms and styles of worship and living. It's quite right for you to find the one that best fits your temperament and taste. Some are stately and subdued, some are cozy and zealous, some are even rollicking and boisterous. Within their diversity, all may be faithful to their Lord. Your friend may like the meditative kind, you the jubilant kind. Most churches have variety within their own histories, but differences persist. The Quakers are not likely to sing uproarious hymns.

If your church is going through a cheerless period, or if present conditions prevent you from being edified, ask yourself some hard questions. Could it be that your discontent is more with yourself than with the church? The axiom, "You get out of it what you put into it," may be too simple an explanation for your uneasiness. But it is true that one person's faithfulness and enthusiasm can become a contagion. It's amazing how a whole group can turn from lethargy and discouragement and come alive because of one person who spreads cheer and hope.

Sometimes the block is interpersonal relations. A wall has risen between you and the pastor, or between you and other members. A simple act of kindness could bring you together.

Maybe the pastor does not measure up to your expectations. Could it be that you had become overly attached to some former pastor and you have an emotional problem adjusting to the ways of the new one? Most pastors try earnestly to use the abilities God has given them. Your pastor may have fears and anxieties which he is bravely trying to hide from you. He may need you more than you need him.

Why do we belong to a church—to get something? We belong as an act of thanksgiving to God. At the hour of worship we come to give thanks, not primarily to receive. Of course we expect and need to receive comfort, correction, inspiration, instruction, hope. We are to open our hearts to receive what God may want to give us. Our moods, capricious and often unmanageable, may keep us from receiving what he wants to give. But we can thank him, whatever our moods. And we thank him best by asking him what he may want us to do. In *doing* for him, we open doors to his comfort.

"What's in it for me?" is a shabby basis for choosing a church or anything else. Selfishness is always counterproductive. It puts us on a dead-end street. Joy and contentment lie in a different direction.

And after all, what is your church? It does not belong to the pastor or to the boards or to the choirs. The church belongs to Christ, and you belong to him. In a strange sense, you yourself are the church, at least as much as any other person in the congregation. Don't ever say it's "Pastor Smith's church" or "their church" or even "the church." Say *"my* church."

You may have every right to say, "My church has become a dull place. It's lost some of the zeal it once had, and I have a hard time feeling the joy I should have." But the spirit of God lurks in your church. He waits to fan your languishing spirits into new and joyous life. And the key to just that kind of renewal may lie in your hands.

When You Think You're Not Needed

One of our deepest needs, perhaps the very deepest, is to be needed. This fact is a clue to something essentially fine about us.

To reach a point in life when no one needs us any longer is a frightening prospect. This is a fear for both old and young. Young people wonder if the world will have a place for them. Older people, about to retire, dread the thought that their time of meeting needs will soon be over.

If you gave young people a million dollars each and told them that they must loaf the rest of their lives, you would drive them to melancholy. Show wealthy older people brochures for endless travel, and they lapse into sadness. A friend of mine, recently retired and jetting from one resort to another, said, "Al, these swimming pools get old awfully fast."

I remember well when my sister, the youngest of our family of six, was graduated from college. I told my mother that it must be a wonderful day for her and dad. At long last they were through struggling with college bills. She replied, "We've often talked about that day coming and how nice it would be, but now that it's here, we're a bit sad to think that you don't need us any longer." At the end of another generation it is now my turn for sadness. Our six, too, have finished college.

There are other ways to be needed than paying college bills, of course, or, for that matter, working at a job. My parents lived 21 years beyond my college graduation, and they may not have known it, but in many ways they met my needs as fully then as before. When they died, both the same summer, they left a great ache in my heart and a yawning hole against the skyline of my life.

One of the deceits of our industrial civilization is to measure people's worth in terms of production. If they aren't producing food or shelter, health care or education, or the myriad things people consume, they have a hard time rescuing any sense of importance. They become horses put out to pasture, obsolete machines, wards of the state, parasites on society. A consumerist culture puts them on a shelf to wait the day of the mortician.

Nor will they be rescued by another deceit, such as substituting hobbies and travel for work. That is nothing more than trying to make the shelf more tolerable. They need something else. They need to be needed.

As you grow older, you *are* needed—maybe not in the factory or office or wheat fields or operating room or school room, as you were before, but you are needed by every person who is lonely and discouraged, every person who is forgotten, every person who cries out for someone who cares. And there are millions of such, many in every community, whether they be rich or poor.

He never knew it, but I needed him. He was totally paralyzed with arthritis, lying in his bed like a board. Except for his alert, sparkling eyes and his warm smile, he didn't move, but he had an inner radiance. I never left him but any lingering self-pity was smashed to bits. He put me on my feet again to face life with cheer. He was no obsolete machine. He may never have known how important he was to me and to others, but God knew. It must have been such awareness that led John Milton, blind at 44, to say in his ode, *On His Blindness:* "They also serve who only stand and wait."

For want of imagination, a person may fail to find the doors to others' needs. A pastor told me of a business executive who, upon retirement, was so bored that he kept drinking more and more. His wife soon joined him, and both were well on the way to becoming alcoholics. One day the pastor virtually compelled him to deliver some Meals on Wheels to elderly and sick people in the community. This did it! He became absorbed in the lives of these people who had escaped him during his busy executive days. Meeting the simple need of providing a car for the delivery of meals, he found doors opening for giving himself in ways he had never known. He needed neither hobbies nor travel nor martinis to brighten up his retirement shelf. He was off the shelf.

Jesus gave us the key long ago. "It is more blessed to give than to receive." What sheer fun it is to be able to fill another's need.

In a profound sense, we are of importance not because we are productive, not because we are needed, not because of anything we do or don't do. Our importance is given us as a gift from God. We are his children, loved by him, simply because we exist. We have worth because we *are*. We are justified by grace, grace alone, not by any inventory of works.

But he needs us. He commissions us for a life of service. And his enterprises on earth have myriad openings, for old and young. To let ourselves be needed is to discover the riches of life with God.

When
You
Can't Forgive

I sat with two of my friends. One had grievously wronged the other.

When John said, "I will never forgive you," I told him, "I won't let you say *will never*. I'll let you say *can never,* because on your own I don't think you can. But there is a power that can help you. That's what this whole business of Christianity is about."

I don't know whether he ever forgave, but he understood. He knew that if he were to take Christ seriously, he couldn't decide never to forgive. He had to be open to the miracle.

If I were Jewish and my parents and brothers and sisters had been executed in Hitler's ovens, could I ever forgive? Could I join Jesus in saying, "Father, forgive them; they know not what they do"? Maybe, but if so, it would be a sheer miracle of spirit. More than likely, until I died I'd have to ask Christ to forgive me for not being able to forgive.

Most of us will never have to deal with Hitler. But life will be full of wrongs that hurt, some little, some big. Whether thoughtlessly or deliberately, people will wrong us, and we will wrong them. And every wrong is a link in a chain of bitterness and hatred that binds us and robs us of joy. It's a poison that eats away at our hearts.

There are wrongs so trivial that they need not distress you. Someone seems to snub you. Someone forgot to thank you. They left your name out of the paper. They forgot your birthday. They never sent you a card when you were in the hospital. If you let these little things bother you, you're on the way to what the psychologists call paranoia. You enjoy self-pity. In almost all such instances the oversights were unintentional. Forgive them and forget them.

But there are real wrongs. Your husband becomes enamored of another woman and has an affair. Your wife becomes an alcoholic and your home life is soon in shambles. Your partner in business maneuvers you out of the company. You thought someone was your friend, but you learn that he has misrepresented facts about you to squeeze you out of a job. A relative who could have helped you out of a jam simply let you down.

Evil is afoot in the world, in our hearts and in the hearts of all. There is none really good, through and through. Try as we will, we will struggle with the Mr. Hyde, the dark forces of our natures. Our goals and our motives will be a bewildering mix of the good and bad, the unselfish and selfish. We will wrong others by what we do and by what we fail to do, no matter how vigilant we are.

You dare not set out to forgive someone unless you understand that you too need forgiveness. If you can't admit that you need to be forgiven, any forgiveness you may presume to give will be nothing more than condescension, patronage, at best, pity. From your high and mighty station of purity, you look down (probably with disdain) on the person to be forgiven. This kind of forgiveness is more cruel than none at all.

It was John Bradford who, watching someone being led to the gallows, said, "There but for the grace of God go I." You may not be able to put yourself in the place of persons who have wronged you, but you will need to try— if you are to be able to forgive. What drove them to do these things? Were they more susceptible to such weaknesses than you are? What strengths may the Lord have given you through the years that they failed to develop? Having favored you with strength, does the Lord expect you to carry some of their weaknesses? You can't dismiss the wrong by saying, "They couldn't help it." Nonetheless, people do vary in the natures and heritages and faculties they have.

You might even ask, "Are they happy in what they have done to me?" Who, in the long run, suffers most? When the Scriptures point out that it is better to suffer wrong than to inflict wrong, they direct us to a profound secret of life. What uneasy conscience, what fleeting advantage, what questionable pleasure may come from doing wrong, compared with the profound joys that come from being able to forgive wrongs?

But you ask, "How can I forgive them if they do not want forgiveness?" All you can do is be ready and willing to forgive. Until people face their wrong and show some indication that they want forgiveness and reconciliation, the road is blocked—for them, not for you. You may rid your heart of the poison of resentment, hatred, bitterness, and await the moment when your gift of forgiveness can be delivered.

We'll never get far with forgiving one another unless we understand that we are embraced by our Lord in his love and forgiveness, as wide as the wideness of the sea. If we start there, as the forgiven of God, he can let us in on the joy of becoming the forgiving ones. We may then discover, as George Macdonald has said, that to forgive is the luxury of the Christian's life.

When Grief Won't Let Go

I knew grief when my father and mother died the same summer at 66, but that grief lifted. It was different when our son was killed at 24.

My parents' death left me sad to think that I had no one to write to about the joys of their grandchildren. I realized that now I was on the top rung of the ladder of the generations, and it was lonely up there. I no longer had the luxury of being someone's child.

Twelve years later our Paul's life was snuffed out on a

city street, ten minutes from our home, as he was returning from two years at Oxford as a Rhodes scholar. Accustomed to the reverse flow of British traffic, he stepped in front of a truck. Now I knew a wrenching grief that fastened itself to me like a leech and wouldn't let go. In my 20 years as a parish pastor I had tried to help others with the pain of such festering grief. Now it was my turn to suffer.

Day after day, whenever I wasn't pressed with duties, I'd think of Paul. Never during his two years in England was I so preoccupied with him. Then, though separated by the Atlantic, I took him for granted. Now, separated by death, he became an obsession.

I had my faith. I believed that he still lived, now beyond another ocean. I believed that he was no longer oppressed by pain or meaninglessness or the prospect of death. In a sense, I knew he had "made it" in the fulfillment we all desired. Why then the pain?

A horde of questions attacked me. Like Jacob, who had loved Benjamin more than the others, had I loved Paul more than my other four sons and daughter? Were there things between Paul and me we should have cleared up, had we known the end was so near? What had I failed to do for him? Why should God let a promising young man die?

I felt grief and anger and remorse and guilt and loneliness. I cried to God. He came with comfort, but it took time.

I had the most trouble with my anger. I resented the words of Job, "The Lord gave, and the Lord has taken away; blessed be the name of the Lord." I knew the Lord had given Paul to us, but I couldn't believe the Lord had arranged an accident to take him from us. I found myself angry, not at God, nor at the truck driver into whose path Paul had impulsively stepped. I was angry at the fallen order—in Omar Khayyam's words, "this sorry scheme of things entire," where sin and tragedy and accidents and illness and pain and death can thwart the greater plans of God for his children. I found comfort in thinking that God was indignant with this too, and that in a mixture of love and indignation he had sent his only Son to earth to put in motion a plan that would eventually set things right. I rediscovered a God who suffers with us.

I also learned the loneliness of grief. We are a tightly knit family, and we have a host of warm friends. We shared our grief. But grief leaves you on an island, quite alone. Even his mother and I could not really reach into the recesses of each other's grief. George Macdonald's words from *Diary of an Old Soul* I found to be true:

> We all are lonely, Maker—each a soul
> Shut in by itself, a sundered atom of thee.
> No two yet loved themselves into a whole;
> Even when we weep together we are two.

Guilt was not a serious problem. I could think of nothing serious that had come between us. Even if there were, I quickly reminded myself of the sweeping forgiveness of God that swallows up all our sins and removes them "as far as the east is from the west." Paul, now in heaven, and I, still on earth, could chuckle over anything that had marred our relationship, whatever that may have been.

Still, I felt it was virtually my duty to grieve. If I didn't grieve, had I loved him after all?

The magnificent picture in Hebrews came most to my rescue. In chapter 11 the writer parades the people who have died in their faith and who now, as victors, are in the celestial bleachers cheering us on.

> Therefore, since we are surrounded by so great a cloud of witnesses, let us also lay aside every weight, and sin which clings so closely, and let us run with perseverance the race that is set before us.

I pictured Paul in those bleachers, urging me to drop grief and return with zest to the common life and the joy of those around me.

It isn't as if grief ever quite lets go. But now, except for some swift, unexpected moments, when the loss surges in upon me again, the wrenching pain is gone. Some of life's mirth and merriment may be gone too. But sorrow becomes more like a minor chord in a symphony which, with the jubilant majors, combines to make a rich melody.

We do not belabor Paul's memory, nor avoid it. I occasionally wear his sweaters. We keep his pictures on display. Even his oar is resting against our bookcase, the oar he used in the Henley Regatta in the summer of 1960. It is at Christmas time that we miss him most. There are no presents for him or from him, nor his Christmas letter. We speak of what he might now have been doing. Sometimes I ponder what pain he may have been spared.

The passing of time helps, but it cannot fill the empty place. Fell a great tree, and a hole yawns against the skyline. No one ever takes another's place. All of us have a space in existence all our own. Our loss of Paul is indeed well flanked (12 grandchildren have come since his death). Our other sons do not have their mother's brown eyes and black hair, but they and his sister all reincarnate some of Paul's exuberance and warmth.

When King David's little son was sick, the king fasted and prostrated himself before the Lord, and would not be comforted. The seventh day the child died. The servants hesitated to tell David that the child was dead, fearing that he would do himself harm. To their surprise, when he heard it, David washed himself, dressed, anointed himself, and sat down to eat. He told his servants, "While the child was still alive, I fasted and wept; for I said, 'Who knows whether the Lord will be gracious to me, that the child may live?' But now he is dead; why should I fast? Can I bring him back again? I shall go to him, but he will not return to me."

Paul sleeps in a little windswept graveyard on the prairies of South Dakota, next to his grandfather and grandmother. But he lives on in the fabric of the many lives he cherished and, I believe, ennobled. And with more than wistful longing, I believe that he lives and works in another part of the far-flung empire over which the Creator rules. I will go to him there. It is in the dimensions of that empire that grief comes tremulously to rest.

When You Come in Second

It isn't true that everyone loves a winner. Let us admit that it's not easy to love those who came in first in the race for wealth and power and prestige. If you come in second, you drop back with the rest of us, the losers. We understand you and like you, because you didn't win. In our own way, we'll try to comfort you.

Let's take a look at the people who always *need* to be at the top. If they're students who set out to be at the head of the class, they may fall into some very unappealing ways. They may be secretly delighted when others fail, distressed when other succeed. They may lose their capacity to rejoice with those who rejoice, weep with those who weep. They certainly are not disposed to help someone get on. They may become quietly proud and priggish about their own excellence. They may even become unfair and take unjust advantage of others who are competing.

How about those who strive for excellence but do not need to be first? They use well the gifts God has given them. They are competitive and enjoy others who are competitive. They don't live in fear that someone will be better than they are. They study hard, play hard, and enjoy people. If, at graduation, someone has outdistanced them and is valedictorian, they are genuinely glad to congratulate him or her, because they did not *need* to win.

It may not be quite as simple if you are a contractor and are bidding a job. To come in second is to lose the job altogether. Haven't you known builders who simply move on with "you win some and you lose some," and turn to the next bidding? They have no rancor or bitterness toward the winner.

I've known people running for office who are like that. They give the race all they've got, never stooping to deceit or subterfuge. If they lose, they accept this as part of the process and go on to alternatives of service.

I suspect that people who can take their losses with grace have learned some of God's great lessons. They probably recognize that, with their limited wisdom, they cannot always know what is good for them. They know, too, that God has more than one door to fullness of life and that when one door closes others may be opening.

Victor Hugo tells of sitting in his study one summer day when a bee flew in through the open window and began trying to find its way out again. It flew about frantically, dashing its little body against one pane and another. Victor Hugo picked up a towel and tried to direct it back to the open window. Mistaking his benevolent motives, the bee beat its body against the towel and soared about from one end of the room to the other. At long last, Mr. Hugo got it near the open window, and suddenly, smelling the flowers, the bee darted out to freedom.

To lose the top spot or a contract or an election may in some mysterious way be destiny edging us to an open window. Who knows? The great comfort is knowing that the purpose of life is to be a servant, loving and helping others. This is the one clue Jesus gave for greatness, for winners, if you will.

Living two doors from our home is a man who, in his bid for a second term as governor of Minnesota, came in second by a hair. Far from retreating in bitterness, Elmer L. Andersen discovered many other doors of service to the church and community. He became chairman of the University of Minnesota board of regents, chairman of a great foundation, and finally a newspaper publisher. Another "neighbor," Hubert H. Humphrey, missed the presidency by a scant margin, then returned to the Senate to spend his years as a troubadour battling for causes dear to him, and against the cancer that at last brought him to bay. He received the country's love and such accolades as are given to few presidents. Andersen and Humphrey, both coming in second, did not need the winner's door to reach the road to great service.

When some door closes, God probably won't spend his time stroking your hand and weeping with you. He has better ways to comfort you. He turns you away from your defeat to look ahead, tantalizing you with hope and with opportunities for something better.

Best of all, he reassures you that you are his child, and that if your path should be strewn with what seem to be defeats and failures, he will never let you down, but will be with you all the way until a final door opens and you step out of death into the winnings he has in store for you.

When the Choice Is Unclear

A friend applies for a job and asks you to provide recommendations. You know he is a recovered alcoholic, but fear that if you include that information, he won't get the job. Should you, or should you not?

A house is on fire. The husband can save himself, but he cannot possibly save his invalid wife. Should he let her die, or should he stay and die with her?

A 12-year-old boy was brought into the hospital, his leg riddled with shotgun pellets. Gangrene set in (before the days of penicillin). I watched a tortured father as the doctor faced him with the decision: Should he let the doctor remove the leg?

Several years ago a prominent American churchman and his wife died from an overdose of pills which they had taken in a mutual pact to end their lives when they were no longer able to contribute to the world. Each had become debilitated by an incurable disease that threatened to rob them of intelligence and speech. The whole Christian world puzzled over their choice.

At a conference on Christianity and economic decisions, Arthur Fleming, then chief of the Office of Defense Mobilization under President Eisenhower, asked how the church could help him in the hard decisions he had to make between Sundays. He said it was easy to decide that the Lord wanted him in church on Sunday to worship and to teach a class, to tithe, to have family prayers. But in the complex issues that faced him in his office, he was without clear direction. Who could help him?

Many people make choices with little or no thought for the will of God or even for moral principles. But those who want to do the right when the way is not clear may cry for some cable from heaven.

Are there any guidelines for tough decisions? I think so. Take a good look at the Ten Commandments. They are valid still, after all these centuries. And consult some person of integrity in whom you have confidence. From what you know about the life of Jesus, ask yourself what he would likely do in your situation. You have reason and common sense—use them. Remember, too, that Jesus was hard on the law-and-order boys of his day. Listen to your heart.

To fulfill God's laws, on one hand, and to show mercy to people, on the other hand, can bring us into difficult conflicts. In our complex society, we face baffling choices. We are left without absolutes, except in broad, sweeping principles. Even the familiar "Do unto others as you would they should do unto you" won't always hold. An alcoholic may give a fifth of whiskey to a fellow alcoholic because that's what he'd like to have done for him. That would be a gesture of goodwill, but hardly pleasing to God.

When you have marshaled all the wisdom you can and siphoned off as much self-interest as possible and you make the choice with every good intention, you may still have to be tentative enough to add a little prayer: "Forgive me, Lord, if I have misjudged what you wanted me to do." And he forgives!

When Conscience Seems Too Costly

Martin Luther was 38 when in 1521 he stood trial at the Diet at Worms before the combined courts of the church and the emperor and was commanded to recant. He refused. His conscience would not release him. He knew it would probably cost him everything. The church would excommunicate him, and he would lose his teaching post, perhaps even his life. He said quietly, "Here I stand. I cannot do otherwise."

How does one define conscience? Merely our conditioned response to our environment? Our inner, better self? The voice of God in our hearts? However we describe it, we may think how much easier life would be if we had no conscience to trouble us.

None of us may have to pay the price that threatened Luther, but in all sorts of situations we are faced with choosing the right thing to do, knowing that it's going to cost something.

A mother says no to her daughter, knowing full well that she will misunderstand and be angry. To have said yes would have been much easier. A teacher gives a student a failing grade, when to give a passing grade would have pleased both student and parents. You resist the temptation to withhold something in your income tax report, and you pay a larger tax. You refuse to lie and cover up for a friend who has been dishonest, and you lose a friend.

The whole of organized society is held together by conscience, sometimes called integrity, or trust. To say of a man, "His word is as good as his bond," or "He would rather be right than be president," is to give him high praise. But it's not always comfortable to live that way.

Senator Edmund G. Ross of Kansas in 1868 did what one historian has called "the most heroic act in American history," and one of the most crucial. He cast the one vote necessary to prevent the impeachment of President Andrew Johnson.

The story is recalled in J. F. Kennedy's *Profiles of Courage*. Johnson had sought to follow the healing policies of the assassinated Lincoln, to be generous toward the South, and thus infuriated the majority of Congress that pressed for a hard, even ruthless, policy. Senator Ross was under tremendous pressure to impeach from his fellow Republicans and from his own state. He did not like Johnson, but he saw him being maneuvered out of office by the passions of reprisal of the post-Civil War North, without benefit of a fair trial.

When Ross cast his deciding "not guilty" vote, all the furies descended on him. Not until 20 years later, when passions had abated, did the nation recognize the truth of Ross's words:

> If . . . the President must step down . . . a disgraced man and political outcast . . upon insufficient evidence and from partisan considerations, the office of the President would be degraded, cease to be a coordinate branch of government, and ever after be subordinated to the legislative will.

Ross had saved the genius of our government—the balance among the legislative, executive, and judicial branches. It cost him dearly. He lost his seat in the Senate, and he was reviled by the Northern press as "a traitor, like Benedict Arnold, a poor, pitiful, shriveled wretch." When he returned to Kansas in 1871, he and his family suffered social ostracism, physical attack, and near poverty.

But Ross had the kind of inner comfort God gives. He had been faithful to a trust, true to his conscience.

In Shakespeare's *Hamlet,* Polonius sends his son Laertes on his way with this counsel: "This above all, to thine own self be true, and it must follow, as the night the day, thou canst not then be false to any man."

Decisions of conscience may never be as clear as night from day. They rarely are. But you can do no more than ferret out the issues, rely on your insights of God's will, use common sense, pray, and then let conscience lead.

When You're Expecting a Baby

Who needs comfort when she's expecting a baby? Shouldn't this be a time of joy?

It is, usually, but it's also a time of anxiety. So much is at stake. The desire for a healthy, normal child is so strong that fears creep in. Many a mother waits anxiously for the doctor's assurance, "You have a fine, healthy baby."

There are other anxieties as well. When two people decide to have a child today, they do so with considerable courage. They not only risk having a child who is not normal and healthy, but they also risk all the potential hazards of rearing them in an uncertain world.

Our world seemed safer, for both parents and children. Without knowledge of contraception, my wife and I assumed we were automatically in the business of having children. We never counted the cost, nor seriously considered living without children.

In recent years I've known young people who wonder whether they have a right to bring children into a world such as ours. I think they're mistaken, but I understand. If there's to be an atomic holocaust, why give life to another person to be burned up?

Nor were divorces as common in my day. Now many young couples have friends whose marriages have gone on the rocks and left children stranded. Do they want to risk such tragedy?

Whenever I hear of a young couple who are to have a baby, I applaud them. I am delighted that they're willing to take the risks.

The risks are offset, of course, by the possibility of immense joy. I feel sorry for couples who grow old without children or grandchildren, many of them not from choice nor from the want of courage.

If you didn't plan to have this baby, make up your minds at once that you want this child very much. The moment you look into the face of your very own baby, all misgivings will vanish. And just think—what if you could never have one? I chuckle every time nature (or God) outmaneuvers the pill and tricks someone into having a child.

Nor will it be different if you think you already have your quota, and then suddenly discover you're in business again. Many parents have been grateful beyond words for the "caboose" that brightened their mature years.

What if the child should be mentally or physically handicapped? This is rare, but suppose it should happen to you? Don't fret about this before the child is born. If it should happen, there will be ways to deal with it. Both government and private sources offer much help. And God has ways.

Now that abortion is an option, we speak in new ways of the unwanted child. A girl, perhaps in her teens, is pregnant. Or a family is overburdened with several children already, and the mother is pregnant again. Should they have a right to stop birth?

Without marshalling the many points of view, both pro and con, that may bear on this perplexing issue, I think that, with the large number of good parents waiting to adopt, it would be generous for the mother to refuse abortion and provide a child for those who may be able to give it every reasonable advantage. God gave us life, and we must stand in awe of the gift.

Your child may be another Abraham Lincoln, another Marie Curie. Who knows? Your child may be God's gift not only to you but to the world.

More important still, your child is also God's child, created in your womb in the image of God, destined for a few years here, and to a life everlasting in the imperishable kingdom. God is loaning a child to you for a season. It is your privilege and high honor to care for God's child, and to be profoundly grateful that you have been singled out for this eternal task.

If, like most, you want this child, if you have longed for its birth, you already have dreams for your baby. You have laid plans, and the layette is ready. Grandparents are excited, eagerly waiting. Enjoy these swift weeks before the baby appears. They are good times. Don't let anxieties rob you of the joys of anticipation.

When Fear Paralyzes

Any kind of fear tends to immobilize. In its extreme form, terror, it paralyzes. You can't utter a sound, you can't move.

Most fears are rooted in some circumstance, real or imagined, over which we have no control. A dog leaps out of the bushes to bite, a car veers into our lane, a forest fire sweeps toward us, we are awakened by stealthy footfalls in the dark. The danger is real. We fear.

There are also fears generated by something not

dangerous at all. Small spaces, such as an elevator, make some people tremble. Others fear large spaces, such as prairies. In Rolvaag's *Giants in the Earth,* Berit, the immigrant wife, comes from Norway's mountains to the endless prairies of the Dakotas. She creeps into a large trunk and tells her husband, "Out here there's nothing to hide behind and nothing to lean against."

Others are plagued by a pervading fear, like an overhanging cloud. They don't know why, or where it comes from. They want to escape, but they don't know from what. The fear may be rooted in some forgotten experience in the far past, and expert help will be needed to ferret it out.

My own encounter with fear that makes no sense took the extreme form of what is called "stage fright." As a junior in high school, one day I was reading a part of a Shakespearian play when the thought flashed through my mind, "Suppose I can't finish reading this paragraph." Suddenly I was in panic. I struggled to read on, but ground to a breathless halt.

My panic was senseless. I have good lungs, a good voice, and people are friendly. But from that moment on, through a lifetime, again and again I have fought that fear. In classrooms, as my turn to read approached, I sometimes found some pretext to leave the room. I considered quitting school. When I enrolled in college, I majored in chemistry and mathematics, determined to go into some work where I would not be called on to read or speak in public.

At one point I thought that God might be telling me something. When Paul prayed to be rid of his "thorn in the flesh," God chose to let him keep it, saying, "My grace is enough." Was God giving me one point of stark need, to remind me that in everything I must rely on him?

Though I ended up in an occupation in which I've been reading and speaking to the public most of my life, the fear has never left me. It lurks under the surface every time I face an audience, or even when I read the Scriptures to my family. Its paralyzing power is still there.

I suppose most of us know best the fears of the unknown—of a threatening future, for instance. The fear may be highly personal, such as fear of losing by death or betrayal someone we love. Or it may be more global, such as fearing a future where nuclear war, world hunger, the exhaustion of energy, and overpopulation loom like dark clouds on the horizon.

Ours is an age of that kind of fear. Never before has the world been so interdependent, never before have nations had such power to destroy, and never before have the media thrust these fears into the living rooms of every home. My grandfather, pioneering the prairies a hundred years ago, would read of crises in Moscow, London, or Washington two weeks after the event, and then probably on page three of his Norwegian weekly, without benefit of pictures, and with no effect on his blood pressure. He had blizzards and grasshoppers and drought to worry him, but not the collapse of the world. Hal Lindsey's book,

The Late Great Planet Earth, would not have been on the best seller list 100 years ago, or 50.

Fear breeds hopelessness, and hopelessness paralysis. We are all tempted today to give up on the future, to eat, drink, and make merry in some grim way until the holocaust comes. We drive ourselves with short-range goals, such as making money or gaining power or pursuing pleasure. We wonder if long-range goals—righteousness and justice and purity of heart—have any value. And in the wake of giving up on abiding values, we give up on the dignity of the human being. Short-range passions take over, and unbridled pursuit of power sends six million to Nazi gas chambers. Unchecked clamor for wealth widens the gap between the haves and the have-nots, and unleashed pursuit of pleasure lures our youth to cohabit without marriage, and their parents to drift into divorce courts.

How can God comfort us in this hour? He wants to. His heart must be breaking when he sees his children throwing their inheritance to the winds.

When I look for comfort, I try to remember some basic insights from Scripture. First, God is both merciful and just. If a child has broken the law and lands in prison, a good parent will not break into prison and help the child escape. The child must pay the just penalty. A good God cannot lightly dismiss our sins. Such indulgence would only speed us on to continued destruction. But he is merciful, and of infinite patience. He will not abandon us.

I remember a question from the edition of Luther's

Small Catechism I used as a child: "How does God deal with us in our sins?" The answer given was, "He allows us to sin, but sets limits to our sinfulness."

I think that God is still in control, and that he has ways to turn us in our wretchedness (and history itself) around to a new direction. Evil plants the seed of its own destruction. It's not only the forces of righteousness that destroy evil; evil is self-destructive. The wheels of God grind slowly, but they grind surely.

Then, I dare not minimize the power of one person who is dedicated to God and to service in the world. Goodness is stronger than evil. History has many instances of this truth. Sir William Wilberforce at age 21 was elected to the British Parliament. Three years later he had a decisive encounter with God, and he considered leaving Parliament for "religious work." His friend, Pitt the Younger, persuaded him to stay and struggle politically against the legalized slave trade of the empire. Three decades later, largely through the untiring efforts of Wilberforce, Parliament outlawed slavery and reimbursed slave holders 20 million pounds sterling out of the national treasury.

Who knows where in this very hour God is moving and equipping some individual for work that can reverse the flow of history! All of us have orbits in which we are invited by God to give ourselves to unselfish service for others, in our homes, in our churches, in our communities. Our little battles for justice and mercy may not be as dramatic as that of Wilberforce, but our Lord weaves them into the warp and woof of the whole. We become part of his leaven, that which keeps things from disintegrating and gives hope for the future.

When well-meaning people give up in pious despair and do nothing but sit around waiting for the Lord's return, the Lord must be displeased. We dare not let fear rob us of hope. The earth is the Lord's. This is part of his kingdom. It's not the final fulfillment, of course. He will give us a new heaven and a new earth. When, no one knows. Meanwhile, he has put us here to care for this one, and for one another.

"Let us, then, be up and doing, with a heart for any fate," said Longfellow. There may be catastrophes, there may not. Asked what he would do if the world were to end tomorrow, Luther is supposed to have said, "I would plant an apple tree today." Ignatius Loyola, 16th-century founder of the Jesuit Order, as a student was playing a lawn game with two of his friends. One of them posed the question, "What would you do if the world were to come to the end in two hours?" One said, "I'd go to the temple and pray." The other, "I would go and be reconciled to my brother." Ignatius had been silent. They asked, "What would you do?" He replied, "I would finish the game."

God has put us here in this hour. We have work to do. Putting aside our fears for the long tomorrows, we live in a today throbbing with all sorts of opportunities for service in our little worlds. Remember the words of Hebrews 12: "Lift your drooping hands and strengthen your weak knees . . . . let us also lay aside every weight . . . . and run the race that is set before us."

When You Can't Laugh at Yourself

We all wear masks. We try to be (or pretend to be) something other than we are. In one sense, we are clowns.

There's nothing basically wrong with trying or pretending. Among other things, it's necessary if we are to grow. A child pretends to manage a spoon and spills her food; later she sits down to play her first piece on the piano and strikes the wrong keys. "Don't laugh at her—she's trying," her mother warns.

Laughter, like words, is language. It can be cruel or

126

kind. The moment people laugh they let you into the secrets of their character. If they laugh at your discomfort or your pain, they tell you that they disdain you, or at least that they're insensitive. If, on the other hand, they laugh at their own foibles or embarrassments, even at their limitations and failures, they tell you that they have wisdom and strength and charity. You love them for it.

God must want us to laugh. Only to humans, of all his creatures, did he give the gift of laughter. Not to dogs, not to horses, nor to hyenas. If we can't laugh, we have lost some of our humanness.

To laugh when it's right to laugh and to weep when it's right to weep is to be wise and good. To laugh when you ought to weep or to weep when you ought to laugh is to be a cad or a fool. You wouldn't want to go fishing with someone whose character is that twisted.

People who can laugh at themselves do take themselves seriously, but not too seriously. They understand that there will always be a gap between what they ought to be and what they are, between what they ought to do and what they do. This is essentially a profound religious insight. It is the biblical truth that we are fallen creatures. The human will and mind and emotions have all been damaged by the presence of evil. We are doomed to fall short of perfection, try as we will.

We can find release from the destructive force of this tragic gap by being captured by the great biblical truth that Christ has bridged the gap for us: "Though your sins are like scarlet, they shall be as white as snow." In his mercy God has wiped away the gap, so we can stand before God as if we were perfect.

But only before God. Until we die, we will struggle with the gap that yawns between what we ought to do and what we do. We will yield to temptations, losing our tempers, neglecting our neighbors, becoming defensive, yielding to self-pity, blaming others.

We can deal with this gap in two ways. We can grieve over it, and we should. And we can chuckle over it. We can laugh at ourselves. This is the sense of humor the Lord wants us to have. Laughter is the release valve to the tragic. Tragedy and comedy are two sides of the same coin.

In some areas of life it's more difficult to manage a sense of humor. The Christian faith is one. Over and over again, throughout history, people have pretended to have *the one truth* and have been totally without humor in dealing with others who lay claim to having the truth. Christians have been separated from one another, churches have been riven, wars have been fought—all because people lost sight of the gap between what a person may know and not know. Few theologians have been able to laugh at themselves as they attempt to define religious truth.

Karl Barth, an eminent 20th-century theologian, may be an exception. He is able to chuckle over his efforts:

> The angels laugh at old Karl. They laugh at him because he tries to grasp the truth of God in a book of dogmatics. They laugh at the fact that volume follows volume and each is thicker than the previous one. As they laugh, they say to one another, "Look!

Here he comes now with his little pushcart full of volumes of dogmatics." And they laugh about the men who write so much about Karl Barth instead of writing about the things he is trying to write about. Truly the angels laugh.

Politics is another area in which humor is sparse. Few people are able to take a serious position in the political arena and, in arguing or discussing issues, back away from their seriousness to chuckle over their doctrinaire opinions.

Humor is difficult, too, for those who experience loss of security. To lose one's farm or one's investments—this is serious business. Not many people are able to say with Job, "Naked I came from my mother's womb, and naked shall I return." To relax and say, "The money was never really mine in the first place," and to go on without being crushed, is to have a wisdom that only a religious sense of humor can provide.

Life is full of situations less critical than one's religion or one's security. You have weaknesses and foibles; others have them too. You should be able to laugh at your own, and look with charity at the ones others have. I like these lines from Kipling's *If:*

If you can keep your head when all about you
Are losing theirs and blaming it on you;
If you can trust yourself when all men doubt you,
But make allowance for their doubting too;
If you can wait and not be tired by waiting,
Or being lied about, don't deal in lies,
Or being hated, don't give way to hating,
And yet don't look too good, nor talk too wise;
Yours is the earth.

Archbishop Fischer, late of Canterbury, had the light touch a sense of humor bestows. Upon his retirement, he said that most of his life he had been able to get up in the morning with anticipation to discover what bad news the morning mail might bring, but that now, having lost a little zest for it, he thought he ought to retire. He was able to laugh at himself and to deal in a spirit of humor with the limitations of others.

In his fascinating book, *Scaramouche,* Sabatini describes his gallant Frenchman: "He was born with the gift of laughter, and a sense that the world was mad." Sabatini's young nobleman moves through a world of intrigue with unparalleled courage, integrity, and charity, but always as if quietly laughing at himself and at the world around him. With a saving sense of humor, he is never a cynic.

It may be that genuine, healing laughter can come only with an honest appraisal of the human beings God has created—made in the image of God, yet fallen creatures, the victims of their own wretchedness and foolhardiness. In the gap between these poles is the tragedy and comedy of the human life. Deep down, we know we belong at the heights with God, and in our own blundering, rebellious, and blind way we're trying to climb back up. We weep for —and laugh at—ourselves.

The only way we can laugh with charity, both at ourselves and at our world, is to remember that the God who gave us life and who has redeemed it understands us, and that he lets us use this priceless gift of laughter to give the journey back to him a touch of merriment.

When You're "Only" a Homemaker

Today fewer than 16% of American families have a full-time homemaker-mother. I have no statistics for 50 years ago, but I suspect the percentages would be at least reversed—more than 80% of homes with full-time mothers.

Some believe this shift means progress, that these benighted 16% who still are imprisoned as wives and mothers are the unfulfilled women of our land, and that the 84% are liberated, happy, and productive. But it is tragic

131

when a wife and mother must be embarrassed to admit that she is "only" a homemaker.

Of course there are mothers who find it necessary to work outside of the home. All honor to them! Their husbands are without employment or have abandoned the family. Others find it necessary to augment their husband's modest income to provide funds for their children's education. Many of these women would prefer to be "only" homemakers.

But the temper of our times have led a host of others to conclude that only by having another career can they find fulfillment or be considered productive. This is sheer nonsense.

The family is the basic unit of civilization. Governments, industries, culture, education—everything builds upon what the family alone can provide. God may very well measure how well a man does as a father and husband more important than how he does as president of the United States or of Chase National Bank. It could be that the greatest long-range peril of our age is not the bomb or the exhaustion of natural resources, but the erosion of the family. If the family fails, civilizations most likely won't be worth continuing anyway. Let the bombs fall!

My wife is the mother of our six children, and she and I each had mothers of six. Together these three mothers launched 18 into lives of happiness and productivity. Each prepared at least 150,000 meals, told hundreds of bedtime stories, led countless prayers, nursed children through recurrent illnesses, and all the while let their husbands lean on them for strength and love. I would be enraged if someone were to suggest that their lives would have been more significant had they managed corporations or written books or performed surgical operations.

In our day there will be many mothers who, when their children are grown and have left home, will turn to some career. Let this be the frosting on the cake for them. Until they die, their most important careers will still be to mother and grandmother the next generations into lives of courage and faith and love.

When You Can't Let Money Go

He said with a note of sadness, "I can't let go of my money." He knew he should. He had far more than he would ever need. From the time he was young he had worked hard, been frugal, bought land, invested in fortunate stocks. He had watched himself become wealthy, almost as from the sidelines.

He had never let money go except to have it multiply and accumulate. Now, visiting with a friend who was having a rollicking time giving away his money, he was wistful. He knew he was missing some fun. But he was trapped. His money now controlled him.

Mr. X is not a fictitious character, nor is he alone. Many people—good people—have let themselves become totally arthritic with their money. They began as accumulators, were successful, and continued, until the spiritual muscles that at one time might have learned the joys of distribution had become atrophied.

When J. D. Rockefeller as a young man of 19 was earning $3.50 a week as a bookkeeper, he regularly gave 35¢ a week to the missions of his church. His accumulations became massive, and so did his benevolences. Who knows, he may have had more joy from his distributions than from his accumulations.

It's well to flex the muscles of giving early, long before there's any large amount to distribute. Letting money go for the church and for the many causes that make our common life better brings a unique kind of joy. You shouldn't miss it.

When You Fear Catastrophe

An eminent psychiatrist friend of mine once said that everyone lives with a sense of imminent catastrophe. Any moment one's world could fall apart.

In recent years I've sometimes awakened in the morning wondering whether the world would hold together another day. The problems are so great and the world so interrelated that if one part collapses, won't the whole structure crumble, like a house of cards, into total chaos? In this mood I dress, go to the kitchen for a cup of strong coffee, and read prayers that others have written (I couldn't put together a cheerful one for myself). By the time I get out with other people I have a feeling that the world will hold together, at least for another day.

Don't we all live with a feeling of catastrophe around the corner? My friend is right. A heart attack could fell me. I could get a telephone call that one of my children or grandchildren has been killed.

We were totally unprepared that night of August 18, 1960, when two policemen came to our door to tell us our son Paul was killed. In the years following, whenever our children and grandchildren are due to arrive, I'm a bit uneasy until they're at the door, and when they leave I'm nervous when the telephone rings until I know they're safely home.

It's not that I'm semi-paralyzed, thinking of the worst that could happen, but tucked down somewhere in my consciousness is the awareness of the uncertainties of life.

Nor was it Paul's death alone that brought this awareness of the catastrophic. I was 17 when five of the seven banks in Sioux Falls closed their doors in 1923. That same year my father's store burned to the ground one dry, October night. In 1929 the stock market crash sent the country and the world into unprecedented hard times. And during the war in the '40s I shared the fears of families in my congregation who lived daily with the dread of a telegram: "It is with deep regret that the office of the U.S. Army informs you that your son. . . ."

The world has always lived with the sense of possible

calamity. But it seems to me that in the last three decades, in spite of unrivaled economic affluence in our land, the fear of both domestic and worldwide collapse has been fueled in new ways. I'm not at all sure why this should be so.

The nuclear bomb is new, of course. Thousands of Hiroshimas could mean the end of civilization. Recent calculations of how soon the earth will run out of life-sustaining energy, water, air, and food also create a sense of looming disaster. Then there are the religious "readings of the times," such as Lindsey's *The Late Great Planet Earth,* which carelessly use Scripture to spell doom.

It is an offense to God to give up hope and to live as if our history is but one catastrophe after another building up to one final, colossal holocaust. Anticipation of Christ's return and a "new Jerusalem" comes not from weariness with struggling against the evil forces in this world. It comes from the promise that this world at its very best is but a glimpse of something infinitely more fulfilling to come. Longings for God's heaven come not from a repudiation of God's earth, but from hunger for the goodness and beauty that we have tasted here.

It is unworthy of us as Christians to be apostles of doom, always looking into the tomorrows of impending misfortune. Misfortunes will come, but they need not spell collapse. Most of our fears do not materialize. When they do, we are not abandoned. God is with us, and as he told the apostle Paul, "My grace is sufficient." With him we will weather the storms. Even if the world blows up, it is not the end. We are eternal beings. He who raised up Jesus will raise us up (if we will let him) and give us life anew in the more glorious sector of his kingdom.

We are not wise enough to know that the world is on a roller coaster to disaster. There may be golden days ahead, before Christ returns. The age-old enemies—disease, hunger, and war—may lose some of their power.

Will Durant, renowned historian-philosopher of our century, on his 92nd birthday deplored the decline of religious belief and of the disciplines of our earlier rural society. He struck a final note of courage, however:

> I will not end on this plaintive note. I still believe in you (in people) and in America and in Europe. . . . I believe that there is a creative spirit in the universe —in every atom, in every plant and animal, in every man and woman—a spirit evident in history, despite every setback and disaster. I believe that the human heritage, in technology, government, education, literature, science, and art, is greater than ever before, is better protected, and widely spread, than ever (*Saturday Review,* Jan. 7, 1978, p. 5).

Whenever the dark moods overtake me and the future looms with possible catastrophes, I look back over the years, my own and the world's, and I see how, when we've stumbled, God puts us on our feet once again. I echo the refrain from Cardinal Newman's hymn, *Lead, Kindly Light:* "So long thy power hath blest me, sure it still will lead me on."